A Layman's Commentary

Volume 4

Books
of the
Major and Minor Prophets

Isaiah, Jeremiah, Lamentations, Ezekiel, Daniel,
Hosea, Joel, Amos, Obadiah, Jonah, Micah, Nahum,
Habakkuk, Zephaniah, Haggai, Zechariah and Malachi

John Devine M Eng Sc

BALBOA.
PRESS
A DIVISION OF HAY HOUSE

Balboa Press books may be ordered through booksellers or by contacting:

Balboa Press
A Division of Hay House
1663 Liberty Drive
Bloomington, IN 47403
www.balboapress.com.au
1-(877) 407-4847

ISBN: 978-1-4525-1270-9 (sc)
ISBN: 978-1-4525-1273-0 (e)

Printed in the United States of America

Balboa Press rev. date: 01/14/2014

CONTENTS

Books of the Prophets

Introduction – With the change from **Theocracy to Monarchy** in 1050 BC resulting from the request of the people of Israel for a king there was a need for three positions of authority -

King – appointed to govern and defend the people

Priest – the representative of the people before God

Prophet – one who spoke the Word of God directly to the people and king.

The role of the prophet was to teach the people about God's Law's and to encourage them in their relationship with God. They were to warn them when they were disloyal to God and also to predict things to come, particularly in regard to judgment or deliverance. People often turned to the prophets when there was trouble or when decisions had to be made. Prophecies could have current as well as future application – both in the short and long term. Many prophecies are still to be fulfilled in the long term particularly concerning the end time, the Day of the LORD and the future role of Israel.

A prophet was called by God often from humble circumstances and recognized by the relevance and accuracy of the words he spoke Deu 18:22. They frequently spoke and acted in conflict with the establishment. They were persecuted for their unpopular messages which are still valid today because God's character has not changed – nor has the frailty of human nature.

Jesus has all three of these positions of authority – the perfect Prophet, Priest and King Heb 1:2; 9:11; Rev 19:16.

The last seventeen Books of the Old Testament are prophetic. The first five are called 'major' due principally to their volume. There are many prophets in the Bible record apart from these 'writing' prophets including Moses, Samuel, Nathan, Elijah, Elisha and David.

The writing prophets spoke to the people of Judah and Israel for 300 years through the divided kingdoms and beyond the Exile and return (760-430 BC).

The United Kingdom of Israel Over a period of 120 years Israel was integrated under the reigns of Saul 1050-1010 BC, David 1010-970 BC and Solomon 970-930 BC.

The Divided Kingdom At the end of the reign of Solomon the kingdom was divided due to Solomon turning away from God in his later years 1Kin 11:9-13.

The southern kingdom of Judah retained the capital of Jerusalem and the Temple and survived for 343 years until taken into exile by Babylon 586 BC.

The northern kingdom of Israel established a new capital, first at Shechem, then at Samaria. Because of their rebellion against God they were conquered by the Assyrians after 208 years and dispersed among the nations 722 BC.

The twenty kings of Judah were all descended from the royal line of David continuing the linage to the birth of Jesus Mt 1:6-17; Lk 3:23-32. Eight of the kings of Judah carried out some short term reforms.

God's judgment came first on Israel because all nineteen of the kings were evil (ref p105).

The prophetic writings began possibly with Hosea and Amos after some 170 years of deterioration in both kingdoms. The messages were often repeated and collated so they are not always in chronological or free-flowing order.

The Messiah (Hebrew), Christ (Greek), Anointed One (English) The people of the Old Testament looked forward to an Anointed One, a Savior who would come from God and put all things right. He was seen as the **'Hope of Israel'** Acts 28:20.

He would be prophet, priest and king. All nations of the earth would be included in his eternal kingdom and blessings. He will establish a reign of righteousness, justice and peace Is 11:1-9.

The Messiah was predicted by all the major prophets – Isaiah 9:6,7; 11:1-10; 12:1-6; Jeremiah 23:5,6; 33:14-17; Ezekiel 34:23-31 and Daniel 9:25-27 - as well as some of the minor prophets Mic 5:2,5; Zec 3:8,9; Mal 4:2,5,6.

Jesus Christ, the Messiah Jesus was recognized by many during his ministry to be the **Messiah** Jn 1:49; 4:25,26; Mt 16:15-20; 21:4-11; Mk 11:8-10. He acknowledged himself to be the **Son of God, the Christ** – this was the only reason for the crucifixion Mt 26:63,64; Mk 14:61,62; Lk 22:70,71; Jn 19:7. Followers of Jesus look forward to his Second Coming to fulfill the predictions of the prophets Lk 24:44,45 and to bring in the new eternal kingdom he announced Mt 4:17; Jn 14:1-4.

God's plan of salvation for mankind Throughout the writings of the Prophets the unique message of forgiveness of sins and the gift of eternal life through the Messiah is consistently inferred.

Isaiah – Salvation is of the LORD

Introduction – Isaiah was born around 770 BC and prophesied over 50 years in Judah under five kings. Assyria dominated the Fertile Crescent from 885 BC. Israel fell to Assyria in 722 BC. Isaiah foretold this for eighteen years beforehand. Babylon then controlled the Mediterranean from 600 BC. Isaiah foretold the fall of Jerusalem and the exile of the people of Judah to Babylon which occurred in 586 BC 100 years after his death.
Judah is called Israel, House of David or Daughter of Zion. Israel is called Ephraim after the largest tribe.

Author – Isaiah, prophet of Judah from 740–690 BC.
Period – during the reigns of Uzziah, Jotham, Ahaz, Hezekiah and possibly Manasseh. He was a contemporary of Micah in Judah and Hosea in Israel.
Theme – **The nature and character of God** The glory, holiness, righteousness and justice of God. The chosen people did not honor God or live by his laws. Isaiah repeatedly warned of **inevitable judgment** on atheism, godlessness and rebellion, self-centeredness and social injustice. He reminded them that obedience brings blessing – disobedience brings disaster.
After exile a remnant would return as a unified nation.
The Coming Messiah - God revealed through Isaiah that the Messiah would not be the political leader like the people were expecting but a **'Suffering Servant'** who would deal with the sins of mankind. The kingdom of God would not be a physical nation but an eternal kingdom of 'new people'.
Isaiah contains amazing and specific details of the coming of the Messiah and his work which were fulfilled over 700 years later in the life of Jesus. The first 39 chapters pronounce judgment. The last 27 chapters proclaim salvation and a universal Savior – the same division as the Books of the Bible.

SUMMARY
The Vision of Judgment and Redemption 1:1-31
The Day of the LORD 2:1 to 5:30
The Call of Isaiah 6:1-13

THE VISION OF JUDGMENT and REDEMPTION

1:1-17 Israel and Judah Rebelled Against God Although God provided their daily needs - life, sustenance, rain, sun, prosperity - the people failed to live by his universal moral order as revealed in the Covenant Conditions - they lived proud, self-centered lives ignoring social justice - they rebelled turning their backs on God - they spurned him! v4.

They had a form of religious observance but were living evil lives v16,17.

1:18-20 Reasoning with God The moral order in the heart of man demands that there be justice in the world. Injustice requires discipline Rom 2:14,15. However God is loving and merciful. While the people deserved punishment, if they repented they would receive cleansing – **scarlet sins washed white as snow**. Why do we continue to ignore God? 55:6,7.

This cleansing was ultimately accomplished by God through the sacrificial death of Jesus to remove the offense of sin Rev 1:5; 7:14. God always promises blessing for obedience and warns of judgment for disobedience.

1:21-31 Zion will be redeemed Despite the rebellion and corruption, after discipline a new order will be established in righteousness. This is God's eternal plan! v27.

THE DAY OF THE LORD

2:1-5 The Mountain of the LORD In the last days the culmination of human history will result in peace on earth and a new kingdom under the rule of God Rev 20:1-4. It has always been God's intention that his people take this message to all people of the world v2. People of all nations will come into it and follow God's ways. They will come with great joy v3.

Justice and peace will reign v4. Isaiah was the first great writing prophet of Judah and from the beginning he foresaw this universal plan of God for the nations.

2:6-22 The LORD Almighty has a day in store Judgment will also come - man will be humbled and the LORD alone will be exalted v12,17. This will usher in the new kingdom.

The sovereignty of God is declared in that man *has but a breath in his nostrils* - it is sobering to reflect that we depend on God for each breath v22.

3:1-26 Judgment The people of Jerusalem and Judah were specially chosen by God and so they would be judged for their rebellion and rejection. Those who are faithful to God and his ways will be saved v10.

4:1 Loss of life, blessing and former privilege will be severe.

4:2-6 Messiah – Anointed One - Christ This is the first direct reference to the expected leader who would come from God to deliver mankind from the fallen state of Eden Acts 28:20. He will establish God's kingdom on earth & will have many titles -

• 'the seed of woman' whom God promised would come to crush the evil one Gen 3:15

• Shiloh - he will be a king of the line of Judah Gen 49:10

• Branch of the LORD - who will reign in righteousness, justice and peace 4:2-6

• Immanuel - born of a virgin - he will be called 'God with us' 7:14

• Prince of Peace - a Son who will govern without end Is 9:1-7

• Root of Jesse - he will be of the line of king David 11:1-11

• Righteous Branch - a King who will reign wisely and do what is just & right Jer 23:5,6

• Messiah - the Anointed One, the ruler Dan 9:24-27

• My Servant, the Branch - will remove sin in a day Zec 3:8.

God always intends the best for mankind 1:19. The fallen state lost by Adam is restored by Jesus Rom 5:12-21. This state will find fulfillment at his Second Coming Is 32:15,20; 55:12,13; Rev 21:3,4. He will restore the fortunes of the people - a prophecy with medium and long term effect – both for Israel & the believing people of the world.

5:1-30 God's Vineyard The house of Israel (both kingdoms, north and south v7) were like a vineyard which yielded bad fruit v2. Signs of God's discipline are the loss of prosperity and security and failure of the elements v6.

The people were the 'garden of God's delight' - he looked for justice and righteousness but found only disobedience v7. This song reveals the compassion and intention of God. The LORD will be known by his justice and righteousness v16. Because the people had rejected the Word of God judgment would come from foreign nations v24,26.

The Call of Isaiah
6:1-13 The Glory of God was revealed to Isaiah in a vision -
• he saw the spiritual realm where God's glory, majesty and holiness are manifest v1; Eph 2:6
• he was overcome by the holiness of God, as are all who encounter his revealed Presence Ex 3:5; Lev 10:3; 20:7; Heb 12:28,29; Rev 4:8
• he was undone, laid bare before the LORD who sees all things - nothing hidden - his pride and self-promotion was stripped v5; Heb 4:12,13. We all need this encounter
• he was acutely aware of his own sin and shortcomings as are all who enter God's Presence
• his sin was immediately removed by the touch of God - he was cleansed, ready for service v6,7
• he heard the cry of the Triune God and responded.
'Here am I, send me!' We also may seek to *enter the Most Holy Place by the blood of Jesus* – to see the glory of God and to respond to his call v8; Heb 10:19.
Isaiah was told that the people would not respond to God's invitation v9.

THE SIGN OF IMMANUEL - 'GOD WITH US'
7:1-9 The coming of the Messiah was announced by reference to an event at the days of Isaiah. Pekah king of Israel united with the foreign king of Aram against Ahaz king of Judah 2Kin 16:5. Ahaz feared Judah would fall. God told him through Isaiah that the oppressors would not succeed because Judah must remain until the Messiah came! Within ten years Israel was conquered by Assyria and dispersed through the world. Their land was inhabited by foreigners. As with all of God's promises this message had to be accepted and acted on by faith v9.
7:10-25 A Virgin will be with Child - a prophecy of the Messiah
The king declined to ask for a sign so Isaiah gave a sign from God – *the virgin will be with child and will give birth to a son and will call him Immanuel v14*. This amazing event was required so that the Messiah

would have the nature of both God and man so he could live a perfect life and die in place of the repentant sinner. The prophecy was fulfilled at the birth of Jesus Mt 1:23; Lk 1:29-38. We now take on the nature of God! This passage is coupled with two other **Messianic Passages** 9:1-7 and 11:1 to 12:6. There are some three hundred references in the Old Testament which were fulfilled in the life of Jesus. The probability of this occurring in the life of one person is incredible. A number are yet to be fulfilled. For Ahab the prophetic sign meant the threat of the northern kings would not eventuate - for the future it confirmed the coming Messiah.

8:1-22 **Judgment on Israel** would be administered through Assyria - this occurred in 722 BC - v4; 7:17-25; 2Kin 17:1-7.

The LORD Almighty is a sanctuary to all who regard him v13.

He is judgment to those who reject him and his ways. God's Word is always a stone that causes those who reject him to stumble v14 – even today.

9:1-7 **A Child is Born - a second prophecy of the Messiah** Amazing detail was given about the physical birth and work of Jesus -
* *He will be called Wonderful Counselor*
* *He will be called Mighty God, Everlasting Father*
* *He will be the Prince of Peace*
* *He will reign on David's throne* **in an eternal kingdom of justice and righteousness.**

These prophetic titles include reference to the unity of the triune Godhead and to the deity of Jesus. They also embrace the deep aspirations of all people for leadership that maintains justice, peace and prosperity in all areas of life. They will come to fulfilment in God's eternal plan for mankind.

9:8-21 Israel was sent a message but they regarded it as of natural causes and it was ignored v8-10. So they would be judged for their rejection of God.

10:1-34 Then judgment will come on Assyria because of their arrogance v5,12 – this occurred in 612 BC. God will preserve a remnant of his people v20.

11:1-9 **The Branch of Jesse** - The prophecies of the Messiah foretold that he would be a descendent of king David, of the line of David (son of Jesse) in fulfilment of the promise of God to David to establish a kingdom of peace on earth Is 4:2; 1Chr 17:11-14. This was still the expectation 200 years after David's death. It was met by Jesus Mt 1:1-17; Lk 3:23-38.

11:10-16 **The Nations will Rally** Fulfilment of this prophecy will be in the new millennium kingdom which will embrace people from throughout the world (the Gentiles, non-Jews) - all who will hope in him v10; Rom 15:12; Rev 20:1-6.

12:1-3 **God is My Salvation** People are in bondage to frustration, anxiety and uncertainty about death. Though many won't admit it we are also bound by sin Rom 3:23; 6:23. It is only the LORD God Almighty Creator of all things who can release from this dilemma. He is the source of salvation to all who turn to him and who put their trust in his Son Jesus Christ Acts 4:12.

12:3 **The Joy of the LORD** To know this salvation is to experience joy which is full, inexpressible and beyond circumstances Jn 15:11; 16:22; 1Pet 1:8,9 - *streams of living water will flow from within Jn 7:37-39.*

12:4-6 Let this be known to all the world People of all nations will sing this song of praise in God's universal kingdom for he has done glorious things Gen 12:1,2.

JUDGMENT ON THE NATIONS

God, Creator of the Universe and All Mankind will execute judgment on all who reject him by the revelation which he has placed in the heart of every person Rom 1:18-20. Isaiah foretold the surrounding nations would be punished because they encouraged Israel's idolatry - this occurred within the next 150 years. Human sense of justice demands that there will be a day of reckoning for all mankind 13:9-13; Rev 6:15-17. The same nations surround Israel with hostility today.

13:1-22 **Babylon** was conquered by the united nation of Media / Persia in 539 BC v17.

14:1-11 **God's Triumph Over Evil** In the midst of judgment God's compassion and his promise of a remnant are declared v1-4. The triumphant song of the remnant is recorded v4-11.

14:12-23 **How you are fallen** This passage against Babylon could also describe the fall of Satan from the presence of God for it expresses the great sin of seeking independence from God Ezk 28:11-19; Lk 10:18. Satan is the source of all evil and his eternal destruction is assured Rev 20:10.

14:24-27 **Assyria** fell to Babylon in 612 BC. Despite all the plans of mankind God's plans cannot be thwarted! We can know that his eternal plan for mankind will be fulfilled Rev 21:3.

14:28-32 **Philistia** Israel's enemy became a vassal state to Assyria under Tiglath-poleser III 720 BC 2Kin 18:8.

15:1-9 **Moab** stood against Judah and was conquered by Babylon under Shalmanesser 722 BC.

16:1-14 As descendents of Abraham on the southern border Moab could have united with Israel but refused.

16:5 **In Love a Throne will be Established** Again the people were reminded that God's eternal kingdom will be established.

17:1-11 **Damascus (Aram or Syria)** was conquered by Assyria under Tiglath-poleser III 733 BC.

18:1-7 **Cush** (Upper Nile) was conquered by Assyria under Sennacherib 701 AD.

19:1-17 **Egypt** was also conquered & came under Assyrian rule 671-652 BC 2Kin 18:17.

19:18-25 **Redemption of the Nations** Isaiah continued to foresee the future redemption of people from all nations in the end time kingdom.

20:1-6 **Egypt and Cush** When Israel fell to Assyria 722 BC vl Judah was told by Isaiah not to depend on these southern powers as allies but they did not listen Jer 43:7-13.

21:1-10 Further judgment against Babylon was predicted v2.

21:11-17 **Edom and Arabia** (south east of Edom) were conquered by Assyria 736 BC.

22:1-25 **Jerusalem** was judged because the people *did not look to the One who made it, or have regard for the One who planned it long ago vll.* This is a warning to the people of our day. Jerusalem fell in 586 BC.

23:1-18 **Tyre and Sidon** were destroyed by Babylon under Nebuchadrezzar II in a thirteen year siege 575 BC.

23:9 **The Nations will be Humbled** From the first act of rebellion and self-promotion to the last, the plans of man are frustrated - this is all according to the plan of the LORD Almighty Gen 11:1-9; Rev 17:13,14; Hab 2:12-14.

THE NEW KINGDOM OF RIGHTEOUSNESS

24:1-23 **Final Judgment** This prophecy speaks of ecological vl, moral v5 and economic v7 degradation which is evident today. Those who honor God, from east and west will be saved v14,15. The powers of the heavens and the kings in the earth below will be punished v21. All mankind will be called to account - then the LORD will reign in the new kingdom v21-23.

25:1-12 God's Plan There is great joy for those who anticipate the coming of the LORD according to *things planned long ago v1*. Medium term fulfilment of these words occurred when the Jews returned to their homeland from Babylon in 538 BC. Again they returned from around the world to reestablish the Jewish State in 1948 after being banished from Jerusalem by the Roman Emperor Hadrian in AD 135. Eternal fulfilment is yet to come when God will swallow up death forever v8; Rev 21:1-5.

26:1-21 You will Keep in Perfect Peace As we commit our ways to the LORD and seek him he keeps us in peace and we realize that *all that we have accomplished you have done for us v12*; 1Chr 29:11-13.

27:1-13 The forgiveness and blessing of the new kingdom are described.

28:1-29 A Stone in Zion People stumble when they deny the truth. The stumbling block in Zion was God's righteous and just ways and offer of redemption v16. Jesus is identified with the stone of stumbling 1Pet 2:6. We do well to respond to the LORD's wisdom v29; 1Cor 1:18-25.

29:1-24 The Siege Foretold Jerusalem will be besieged because of rebellion - they hide their plans from the LORD - act as if they were both the potter and the clay v15,16. Yet the LORD will return suddenly with judgment on the enemy v5-8; v17-24. There is the promise of a redeemed remnant v22,23 - their children will be included - *the work of my hands v23.*

30:1-33 God Speaks to the Present Generation Israel were obstinate children. They made plans without consulting God or his Spirit v1. *The LORD longs to be gracious to you - to show you compassion - Blessed are all who wait for him v18.* He provides his Holy Spirit and wants us to hear his *voice saying 'This is the way, walk in it' v21.* This is made possible today because of the death and resurrection of Jesus Jn 16:13.

31:1-9 The LORD will Shield We cannot depend on the ways of the world. God alone can shield and deliver us.

32:1-20 A Righteous King will rule with justice Former ways will be replaced by new understanding. Noble people make plans today to be part of the eternal kingdom. The Spirit will be poured out upon us v15. The Spirit is available to all who accept Jesus as LORD Acts 2:4,38,39.

33:1-24 The fear of the LORD is the key to this treasure - a rich store of salvation, wisdom and knowledge for those who commit to him v6. There is no hope in the ways of the world v14-16. Kingdom qualities are listed v15,16. God is the only sure deliverer and provider v21,22. We will see the king in his beauty - sickness and sin will be past v17,24.

34:1-17 **The LORD has a Day of Wrath** against the nations of all generations Rev 6:17.

35:1-10 **The Ransomed of the LORD** People of all nations will be called to account for denying the God of Creation. That day will be of great joy for those who have acknowledged God for they will see his glory and splendor. All things will be put right as they enter his eternal kingdom on the 'Way' with singing, gladness and everlasting joy upon their heads! v8,10.

God's Power to Deliver
Chapters 36 to 39 record events in the lifetime of Isaiah and Hezekiah which are examples of the power of prayer and the need for repentance and humility – issues that were central to the message of Isaiah 2Kin 18:1 to 20:19.

36:1-22 **Jerusalem Under Siege** Hezekiah was one of the 'good' kings of Judah. In his fourth year as king 722 BC the Assyrians conquered Samaria, the northern capital and captured the southern cities of Judah laying siege to Jerusalem ten years later.

37:1-38 **Deliverance Through Prayer** Hezekiah went into the Temple to petition God 37:14-20. Isaiah gave him God's reply *'Because you have prayed to me – I will defend this city and save it!' 37:21,35.* History records that Sennacherib returned home and was assassinated by his sons so that the city was miraculously saved v38. We may know that God always answers prayer and will defend us 1Jn 5:14,15.

38:1-22 **Hezekiah's Healing** Hezekiah became critically ill. Through prayer he was granted an extension of life v4. During this period he did not use the time well – he failed to testify to God's healing power and also bore an evil son, Manasseh. Yet the line of Judah was established through him.

39:1-8 **Exile in Babylon Foretold** At the time of his illness Assyria was dominant. Babylon came to power around 612 BC with the fall of Nineveh. When Babylonian envoys came to inquire about his miraculous recovery Hezekiah foolishly boasted about his possessions without acknowledging God's healing. Consequently the Babylonians returned to Jerusalem in later years extracting tribute and taking Hezekiah's descendants captive to Babylon as foretold by Isaiah v5.

THE COMING OF THE MESSIAH

To this point the prophecies were about judgment. From here on the message is about God's glorious future for redeemed people from Israel and from the whole of mankind.

40:1-5 The Glory of the LORD Revealed

• **Return from Exile** - after pronouncing punishment God now provided comfort - he will deliver his people

• **Salvation for the nations** - God's glory will be revealed to all mankind v5. John the Baptist described his mission as a voice in the desert announcing God's salvation for the Gentiles Lk 3:4-6. Jesus continued and fulfilled this announcement Lk 4:14-21.

40:6-31 God's Purposes will be Fulfilled

Confidence that God will deliver his people comes from the understanding of who God has revealed himself to be –

• we know the frailty and finite nature of man v6,7

• the Word of our God stands forever v8

• He will come with power to hold all people accountable for how they have lived, for good and for bad v10

• He provides for his people like a Shepherd v11

• He is the Creator and Sustainer of all the universe v12

• His wisdom, knowledge and ways are above our understanding v13,14 – yet he reveals himself to us

• He is Sovereign over all mankind v21-24

• none can be compared with him – his majesty and power are displayed in the heavens v25,26

• His purposes for the creation will be fulfilled v27,28

• those who wait on him and hope in him will renew their strength – they will rise up as eagles v29-31.

This gives us assurance that his purposes will be completed.

41:1-29 God's People

Abraham became the friend of God because of his faithful response to God's requests. He was the first of the chosen people and received great promises from God v8; Gen 12:1-3. Those who are faithful to God will be redeemed v14. While these promises applied directly to Israel they also apply to believers under the New Covenant Gal 3:14.

THE SERVANT OF THE LORD
Having announced the future kingdom God revealed to Isaiah how it will come about.
There are four 'Servant of the LORD' passages -
1. **His Nature** - humble, gentle, faithful, capable 42:1-9
2. **His Mission** – he will restore Israel and be a light for the Gentiles bringing salvation to the ends of the earth 49:1-7
3. **His Commitment** – he will be a servant to deliver his people, providing an example for us to follow 50:4-10
4. **His Sacrifice** – he will suffer, to pay the price for others, to remove the offense of sin 52:13 to 53:12
These prophetic statements were contrary to everything expected. All found fulfilment in Jesus.

42:1-9 **THE SERVANT OF THE LORD 1** Israel saw the Messiah as one who would conquer foreign powers. They did not expect a **'Servant Leader'** who would first be humble, gentle and caring v2,3 - who would set a new standard for the spirit of the Law v4, Mt 5:17,18 - who would *be a covenant for the people and a light for the Gentiles v6* - who would also open blind eyes, free captives and release the oppressed v7.
The Messiah would first have to bear the sins of many 53:4-6. Then he would be the leader and commander of the peoples 55:4. This was a completely new thing the LORD was revealing v8,9.

42:10-13 **A New Song to the LORD** Confident that God will complete his purpose for mankind Isaiah sang a new song of praise to the LORD which one day will be sung from the ends of the earth v10-17.

42:14-25 **Many Will Not Hear** Based on past experience it was prophesied many would not take notice of this Plan of Salvation v18-25;53:1-12.

43:1-7 **The LORD Has Redeemed You** Mankind was created with the intention of redemption v1. God protects his people so they can complete his plan for they are precious and honored in his sight v2-6. This applies to *everyone who is called by my name, whom I created for my glory v7*!
This promise has specific fulfilment for the people of Israel since May 14, 1948 when the state of Israel was proclaimed and also for the end time Jer 31:33,34; Rom 11:26.

43:8-13 **His Witnesses** We are chosen to be witness to his glory and mercy.

43:14-28 The past will be forgotten and everything will be new v18,19. We know we were **formed for God that we may proclaim his praise** v21. Sins could only be forgiven ultimately by the death of Jesus v25.

44:1-6 **Your King and Redeemer, the LORD Almighty** There will be great blessing - the Spirit will be poured out and the people will gladly honor the name of the LORD v3-5 – the LORD will achieve this v6.

44:6-21 **The First and the Last** v6 This name is used of the Father Ex 3:14; Rev 1:4,8; 21:6 and of Jesus Rev 1:17; 2:8; 22:13. The god's and ideologies of man will be seen to be worthless v9-20. We must beware of rejecting gods of our own image without considering the God of revelation.

44:22,23 **God took the initiative** - *I have swept away your offenses - I have redeemed you* - by the death of Jesus v22. As with Israel we have to acknowledge God and return to him to be included in his provision. God displays his glory when we do and causes us to sing for joy as we share his glory! v23.

44:24-28 **God Caries Out His Word - Jerusalem will be rebuilt** As confirmation of the reality of the new kingdom an amazing prophecy was given v26. Assyria was still the world power as Isaiah died. He predicted -
- the conquest of Samaria by Assyria - occurred in 722 BC 8:4
- the fall of Assyrian to Babylon - occurred in 612 BC 10:12
- the exile of Judah to Babylon - occurred in 586 BC 39:6
- fall of Babylon to Media / Persia - occurred in 539 BC 21:9

He now foretold that Cyrus II, the Great, king of Persia would release the future Jewish exiles in Babylon to rebuild Jerusalem and the Temple v28. This event would have seemed incredible at the time of prophecy, before 690 BC but occurred over 150 years later in 538 BC v24-28; Ezr 1:1-4. The return was also revealed to Daniel as a step in the coming of the Messiah Dan 9:25.

45:1-7 **The Anointing** When God chooses a person for his work he provides everything necessary to complete the task. This was true of Cyrus II and the same applies today for those who answer his call! Phil 4:19 -
- the LORD will take hold of our right hand v1
- He will open doors before us that can not be shut v1
- He will go before us and will level the mountains v2
- He promises *'I will give you the treasures of darkness'* v3

- God will strengthen and equip us for whatever he calls us to do for him v5.

I, the LORD, do all these things - bring prosperity and create disaster! v7. We cannot doubt the sovereignty of the LORD - or his provision, in all areas of life Pro 16:9.

45:8-25 **So the LORD will bring salvation** – man cannot question this, as the clay is subject to the potter v8-11. God's purpose will be fulfilled v18. The call to repentance has been given – *turn to me and be saved, all you ends of the earth v22.* God has sworn – *before me every knee will bow; by me every tongue will swear v23,24;* Phil 2:9-11.

46:1-7 **God will Sustain and Rescue You** God not only made us but he sustains us - from birth to old age and beyond v3,4. No other philosophy or belief can offer this assurance!

46:8-13 **Confidence in God** He makes know the end from the beginning - his purpose and plan will stand v10. He will grant salvation to his people v13.

47:1-15 **Babylon Fallen** Babylon rose to power around 620 BC - 70 years after the death of Isaiah. He predicted its downfall in 539 BC 44:24-28.

Babylon, representing the world will be defeated. Our Redeemer, the LORD Almighty will achieve it v4; Rev 18:1-24.

48:1-22 **I will tell you new things** God brought the people into the Promised Land – he taught them what is best for them, he directed them in the way they should go v17. But they rejected him and his warning about disobedience v18.

God the eternal creator will not yield his glory to another – man made or man centered v11,12. The people would soon see the fall of Jerusalem as foretold. These were the former things v3. Now he would tell them new things v6.

THE NATURE OF THE MESSIAH

49:1-26 **THE SERVANT OF THE LORD 2** The second 'Servant' passage explains that the Messiah would come out of Israel. His mission is to bring salvation to the ends of the earth v6; Acts 13:47. He will be despised by nations, honored by kings. Here is great assurance for believers – God has engraved us on the palms of his hands and our children v16-18. God calls us to honor him today then our children will be saved v22,25.

Then all mankind will know that I, the LORD, am your Savior.

50:1-11 THE SERVANT OF THE LORD 3 (third passage) The rebellion by people of all walks of life v1-3 is contrasted with the obedience of God's Servant v4-9. His great suffering was foretold v6 yet he would set his face like flint to complete his mission v7; Mt 20:18,19. We too must fear the LORD, obey his Word and trust in his name v10.

51:1-23 The Eternal Kingdom Israel's heritage began with Abraham and God will fulfill his promises which extend to all nations v4. God's righteousness and salvation will reign forever v8. Ransomed from all nations and generations will enter his kingdom with singing, joy and gladness – sorrow will cease v11. Those who seek God will be vindicated while unbelievers will encounter his wrath v22,23.

52:1-12 Your God Reigns The suffering of God's people for their disobedience will be past. He intervenes – they could not save themselves - now he will pay the price v3. The **Good News** (Gospel) that God will reign in triumph over evil will be proclaimed from the mountains v7. *All the ends of the earth will see the salvation of our God! v10.* Our feet must also proclaim this Good News Mt 28:18-20.

52:13-15 THE SERVANT OF THE LORD 4 (fourth passage) The extent of humiliation and great suffering of the Servant are described – it was required on behalf of many nations who will understand v15; Rom 15:21.

53:1-12 The Vicarious Sufferer (on behalf of me)
These details continue to vividly foretell the pain and suffering of Jesus on the cross -
- Jesus, the Son of God grew up as an ordinary man v2
- He was rejected by his people - few believe him v1
- He was despised, a man of sorrows suffering on our behalf v3
- it was for our sins and iniquity that he suffered and died v4
- it was for us he had to suffer so that we could have peace with God – pierced, crushed, punished, wounded v5
- it was us who deserved the penalty of turning away from God - it was Jesus who had to pay the price v6
- yet he suffered in silence, willingly - a sacrificial sheep v7
- His arrest, execution and burial were foretold in detail v8,9
- this was necessary for the offence of our sins to God to be removed – the atonement – by a sinless sacrifice v10

- He was chosen before the creation of the world for this task of redeeming people from all nations and generations v11,12; 65:1; 1Pet 1:20. The price is paid for all – we only need to accept it!

Following his faithfulness to the call God has exalted him to the highest place in heaven and earth v12; Phil 2:6-11.

Crucifixion was introduced as execution for the first time by the Roman Empire around 150 BC. The Book of Isaiah was included in the Greek Septuagint translation before 250 BC. This reference to crucifixion by Isaiah and connected to Jesus is further confirmation of the veracity of the Word of God.

PLAN OF SALVATION FOR MANKIND Rom 3:21-31

God's Plan of Salvation To understand the need for Jesus to die in our place it is necessary to recognize the awfulness of sin in the Presence of God -

- **God is holy and cannot condone sin** 57:14-16; Ex3:5; 33:19,20 – the absolute moral perfection 6:1-6; Rev 4:1-11
- **The fact of sin** - we are all guilty of sin - falling short of God's glory - his nature and character 53:4; 59:1,2; Rom 3:23
- **The penalty of sin is death** - sin separates from God eternally 53:8; Rom 6:23
- **The penalty for sin has been paid by Christ** - he bore the sin of many - for all who will accept him as Savior and LORD Rom 5:8
- **We are saved by faith** - we cannot save ourselves by our good deeds or philosophies 53:6; Eph 2:8,9
- **You must believe in Jesus as Savior and Lord** v12; Jn 1:12,13 - it was only by his sinless life and sacrificial death that the offence of sin could be removed so that we could be reconciled to God and have eternal life through him.

This explains the devotion believers have to Jesus 1Pet 1:8,9.

This unique plan of salvation is consistently revealed throughout the Old and New Testaments.

- **You must be born again** - Jesus came to make the way for a person to be born into the eternal spiritual kingdom of God 56:5; Jn 1:10-13; 3:1-8. God is Spirit and we who are dead because of sin must be born again of the Spirit of God Eph 2:1-7.

54:1-17 **The Future of the Redeemed will be Great** God, their Maker will be their Husband! v5. He will defend them against all oppression including that of the evil one v16-17. This promise applies to believers today as they embrace and proclaim the good news. We are the bride of Christ Eph 5:2527.

55:1-13 The Universal Invitation God's invitation goes out to all who are thirsty for meaning and fulfilment in life. We are encouraged to seek the LORD while he may be found – to forsake evil actions and thoughts and turn to God who will have mercy and freely pardon v7. Our thoughts are earthbound and finite whereas God has eternal perspective v8,9.
We can depend on God's Word and purpose to be accomplished in full measure and detail v11; Jer 1:12. The eternal kingdom of peace, joy and blessing will be established v12,13.
This was all foretold by Isaiah 66:22; 2Cor 5:21.

56:1-12 An Everlasting Name The outcome of salvation will be an eternity of communion with God v7; Jn 14:1-4. There are others to be gathered even today v8; Ps 85:6-9.

57:1-13 God's Holy Mountain In contrast to the current world order where the righteous perish and people reject or deny God it will be the place where God dwells v13; Rev 21:3.

57:14-21 God Inhabits Eternity Mankind has little concept of existence outside the physical realm. God has revealed himself through his Word as *he who lives forever, whose name is holy v15*. We have to come to grips with this declaration. This high and lofty One dwells with the contrite and lowly v15. He offers restoration to mankind v16-19. It is our privilege to accept this invitation - our folly to ignore it.

58:1-14 Dwelling with the Most High God chooses to dwell, live, reside with those who seek him. He does not accept superficial outward display v1-5 but requires justice and mercy, compassion and righteousness v6-12. We must make the time to experience fellowship with him v13,14.

59:1-21 Sin separates us from God We choose to depart from recognizing him and following his right ways that are best for us. This is the reason for judgment! We must come to acknowledge our sins and offenses, our independence and turning away from God v12,13. Even then we cannot save ourselves – God had to work salvation for all people – by the death of Jesus v16,17.
The Redeemer will come to Zion, to those - who repent of their sins v20. His Holy Spirit alone will change the character and nature of the individual - they will be born of the Spirit v21; 1Pet 1:23. This has relevance for Israel in the last days Rom 11:26.

The Glorious Future for the People of God

60:1-22 When we see the sinful nature of people then and now the glory of the new kingdom causes great anticipation. People of all nations will be included v3. God will be the everlasting light and glory – all things will be made new for the display of his glory v19-22.

THE MESSIAH REVEALED

61:1-11 **Today This Scripture is Fulfilled!** The announcement of the Messiah was proclaimed by Isaiah. He will usher in a new era where suffering, persecution and despair will be replaced by beauty, gladness and praise v1,2.

These words were quoted by Jesus at the very beginning of his ministry declaring his role as Messiah. They were then outworked through his life Lk 4:18,19; Mt 11:4-6 –

• He made *the blind receive sight, the lame walk, those who have leprosy are cured, the deaf hear, the dead are raised and the good news is preached to the poor Lk 7:21-23*; v1,2

• He has given us a garment of praise in place of a spirit of heaviness and despair - we are 'trees of righteousness', planted by the LORD, who display his splendor v3

• He made us priests and ministers of the LORD v6; 1Pet 2:9

• So we may agree with Isaiah - *I delight greatly in the LORD; my soul rejoices in my God v10.*

62:1-12 **Kingdom Watchmen** The day of the kingdom is coming. Those who look forward to it are watchmen who give themselves no rest as they seek to make known the Good News to others. They also give God no rest, at his request, as they petition him in prayer for the salvation of souls v6,7.

63:1-19 **The Day of Vengeance** As in the days of Israel so today many disregard the promise of the day of vengeance and redemption – they think it will not happen v5.

64:1-12 **People cry out for justice** Many continue in the ways of the world as if God has hidden his face v5-7.

NEW HEAVENS and A NEW EARTH

65:1-16 **A Nation That Did Not Call** God in his mercy ordained from the beginning that people from all nations would share in his eternal kingdom. That message has now gone out Mt 28:18-20. However the day of opportunity will end - the day of reckoning will come v6,7.

***65:17-25* The New Kingdom** Although Israel had expectation for the physical Jerusalem the long-range prophecy is for a new order of heavens and earth – a spiritual kingdom where the past will not be remembered because of the joy of the new order 1Cor 15:42-44.

***66:1-24* One Who God Esteems** God will make **new heavens and a new earth** v22. The one who enters will be his esteemed - *who is humble and contrite in spirit and trembles at my word v2*. They will come and bow down before him in an eternal kingdom and possess eternal life v22; 1Jn 5:11,12; Rev 21:1-5.

Good News Isaiah's message outlining God's offer of salvation is available to all who will accept it 1:18-20! Have you?

Jeremiah – 'YHWH lifts up'

Introduction – Born in Jerusalem 656 BC Jeremiah was called by God to be a prophet some 60 years after Isaiah. He prophesied to the people of Judah for over 45 years under 5 kings as their conduct continued to deteriorate. After the destruction of Jerusalem in 586 BC he remained in the city and was then taken to Egypt against his will due to his age and frailty. Jeremiah is an example of a faithful witness under persecution in the midst of an unbelieving community.

The prophecies were often repeated, frequently ignored and are not always in chronological order.

Author – Jeremiah, prophet of Judah from 626–580 BC.

Period – Jeremiah served 17 years under Josiah, a good king. For the next 23 years he spoke against the sins of the people under the last four evil kings leading to the destruction of Jerusalem. He lived in a time of apathy, moral relativity and self-centered materialism.

Theme – Judgment on Judah God's chosen people Israel had become a divided kingdom. Samara in the north fell to Assyria 100 years before. Now Judah was due to face judgment.

Jeremiah warmed the people that their situation was because they had forsaken God and turned from his ways.

The fall of Jerusalem The people should not trust an alliance with Egypt but submit to Babylon for their own good as they were to undergo the discipline of the LORD. It was good advice as Babylon became dominant over Egypt. Had they accepted Babylon's authority they could have remained in Judah in peace.

Jeremiah was a lone voice in the city and was persecuted by the political and religious leaders for his unpopular message. He was ostracized, beaten and imprisoned. He saw the outcome of his prophecies in the fall of Jerusalem and exile of the people. God sometimes calls us to undergo rejection and suffering for the sake of the kingdom but he will supply our needs to complete the task to which he calls us.

Restoration - The Messiah and a New Covenant Throughout his prophecies there was the offer for the people to repent and be restored showing the continual mercy and patience of God against the persistent attitude of the people to turn their backs. He foretold that God would make a New Covenant and raise a righteous King who will do what is just and right 23:5,6; 30:9.

SUMMARY
Call of Jeremiah 1:1-19
Judgment on Judah 2:1 to 15:21
The Sovereignty of God 16:1 to 22:30
The Righteous King 23:1 to 28:17
Seventy Years of Exile 29:1-32
Restoration 30:1 to 33:26
The Final Days of Jerusalem 34:1 to 45:5
Judgment on the Nations 46:1 to 52:34

The Call of Jeremiah

1:1-10 **Before I Formed You - I Knew You** Jeremiah was of a priestly family near Jerusalem. He learned that his life had been planned before he was born v5; Ps 139:13-16; Acts 17:26. This is great encouragement to trust God as he has a plan for each one of us and he knows what is best for us Rom 8:28-30.

Jeremiah felt inadequate for the task v6. Humility is a sign that we are ready for God's use - *my power is made perfect in weakness 2Cor 12:9.* He was told not to see himself as a child because he would receive everything he needed including the words to speak! v7-9. We have this same promise from Jesus Mt 10:19,20; Jn 14:26.

His task was to foretell the destruction of Judah and the surrounding nations. He was also to build up and plant - to confirm the coming of the Messiah with a new order v10.

1:11-19 **The Word of God** In preparation for service Jeremiah was shown two important truths -

• **the branch of the almond** (sounds like watching) explains that God watches mankind to make sure his Word is fulfilled. We can confidently put our trust in God's Word Is 55:11

• **the boiling pot** represents Jerusalem and the surrounding nations under the destructive forces of Babylon. This occurred within 40 years. The message would be resisted but Jeremiah need not be afraid for the LORD will defend him v17-19.

Judgment on Judah

2:1 to 3:5 Israel began as a devoted people under God's protection 2:1-3. But they turned to idols, trusting in their own ability and worldly ways 3:13. They lost their awe of God! 2:19. For this reason the rains where withheld 3:3. They had a form of religion but were doing evil 3:5.

3:6 to 4:41 The northern kingdom of Israel had been conquered some 100 years before (722 BC) and the people dispersed among the nations despite repeated warnings from the prophets. Judah did not learn from this and were pursuing the same path. God called them to return to him and he would have mercy 3:12. If they repented, even a remnant, he would bless them – treat them as a Father treats his sons 3:17-19. Words of confession were supplied 3:22 but they must take action to break up their unplowed lives and stop sowing the seeds of the world 4:3. If they did not repent they would be conquered and exiled in Babylon.

5:1-31 **Not One Righteous** It is difficult to understand how God's people could have departed so far from their commission at Mt Sinai Ex 19:3-6. This is a warning to the Christian nations, people and churches of today. Jeremiah could not find one person who sought honesty and truth v1. The sins of the people and pending judgment were described.

6:1-30 **The Siege of Jerusalem** The severity of the coming attack on Jerusalem was foreseen. This was intended to make the people reconsider their ways but they failed to do so v16.

7:1-34 **Worldly Worship and Evil Actions** People saw the Temple, priests and services as security. They had an outward form of religion but were not walking daily in the ways God had required – they ignored God 2Tim 3:5. He would therefore destroy the Temple as he had done to the Tabernacle at Shiloh in similar circumstances 1Sam 4:22; Ps 78:60. Their worship involved idols and worldly practices and they did opposite to the commands they had been given v23,24. So their places of worship would become a valley of slaughter v30-34.

8:1-21 They were living by their own wisdom – the extent of their sins and the judgment were further outlined.

9:1-26 **Refining and Testing** Jeremiah expressed sorrow at the coming suffering v18,21. The main sin was that they rejected God instead of understanding and embracing his kindness, justice and his righteous ways v24.

10:1-25 **The Glory of God** His nature is revealed – all power, King of nations, Eternal King who made the universe and controls the elements v6-13. Instead of revering God they worshiped idols of wood. We recognize that man does not have the ability to direct his own steps v23; Pro 20:24. Even today world leaders are in crisis and people live for themselves – we need the correction and direction of a loving all knowing God.

***11:1-23* The Covenant Broken** God's Covenant at the time of Moses and renewed a number of times contained blessings for obedience and curses for disobedience Deu 28:1-68. As the Covenant was now broken by the people the curses would result v8. The local leaders hated the message and planned to kill Jeremiah but the LORD protected him v18.

***12:1-17* *They will wear themselves out but gain nothing* *v13* Jeremiah asked the LORD about the evil conduct of the people – *You are always on their lips but far from their hearts v2*. God answered that they would be punished but a remnant would be returned v7,15. There is a warning to all who enjoy God's blessings but deny his commands – *if any nation does not listen, I will completely uproot and destroy it, declares the LORD* v16.

***13:1-27* The case for justice was stated and the consequence. Aspects of punishment included bondage (a belt) v1, correction (a wineskins) v12 and oppression (captivity) v15.

***14:1-22* A drought and destruction - death, starvation and exile will come on Judah. Jeremiah pleaded for mercy but the time for repentance was past and the day of reckoning had come.

***15:1-21* As a result of continued rejection of God by the people the punishment & reasons are further explained. Jeremiah asked for relief from his own suffering. The conditions were the same - if he did as requested he would continue as God's prophet.

THE SOVEREIGNTY OF GOD

***16:1*-21 The Day of Disaster** It was time to refrain from normal activities because the time of judgment was near.
Yet there would be future restoration for a remnant v14,15.

***17:1-8* Two ways of life were described –
• *cursed is the one who trusts in man - and whose heart turns away from the LORD v:5; Deu 28:15-68*
• *but blessed is the man who trusts in the LORD whose confidence is in him v7; Deu 28:1-14*.

***17:9-27* The Human Heart is Deceitful** – with the tendency to do wrong - we cannot know it! Pro 16:25. We do not have to be taught how to do wrong - to do what is right is often a struggle against our human nature. We easily rationalize our behavior. Corruption in leadership occurs in all societies. The rise and fall of empires are confirmation of this truth.

The heart and mind are examined by God and our sense of justice demands that we will be recognized and rewarded according to our conduct and deeds Ps 139:1,23,24. The Sabbath was a special day to relate to God and required to be kept.

18:1-23 **The Master Potter** As clay in the hands of the potter so are all people in the hand of God. We must respond to his leading and shaping as he moulds us to his will and for our own good. To be shaped by the master potter results in a vessel for noble use 2Cor 4:7; 2Tim 2:20.

The people saw the prophetic message as interfering with their self-centered lives and independence from God. They were consumed with a material world and secular society, preoccupied with self-indulgence v12. The challenge to return to the foundation of honoring God and obeying his law disturbed their comfort zone. This applies to the world of today. We forget that all things have come from God! Is 26;12.

They rejected his instruction and planned to attack Jeremiah v18.

19:1-15 Judgment was further described. Clay was made into a pot that was broken indicating the pending fate of Judah.

20:1-18 The Temple administrator had Jeremiah beaten and restrained in stocks. Again Jeremiah sought comfort from God. Yet he could not stop speaking what God had instructed.

His Word is in my heart like a fire - shut up in my bones v9. May our love for knowing and sharing God's Word be fire in us!

21:1-14 As the conquest by Babylon approached Jeremiah was asked to change his message. But he could only speak as the LORD led him – the people were given an option – death or captivity v8,9. They would be punished as their deeds deserved.

22:1-30 Judgment would be severe against those who led the people astray – it will be the same of all generations.

THE RIGHTEOUS KING

23:1-40 **The LORD Our Righteousness** The main cause for the failure of Israel and Judah was the kings and shepherds (leaders, priests and false prophets) who led the people astray v1,15. After judgment on the current evil leaders God promised a righteous king who will reign wisely and bring peace v5 - he will be called *the LORD Our Righteousness* v6. This refers to the Messiah and was fulfilled in the person of Jesus.

He will come again to rule all nations with righteousness! Rev 19:11-16. Then there will be no more scattering shepherds or false prophets v9. **The LORD who fills heaven and earth** will accomplish this according to his eternal plan v24.

24:1-10 **Two Baskets of Figs** Jehoiachin king of Judah was taken into exile in 598 BC 2Kin 24:1,12. The final king Zedekiah was told – those who go into exile willingly will be protected (good figs) – the king and those who resist exile will be destroyed (bad figs). This occurred in 586 BC.

SEVENTY YEARS IN CAPTIVITY

25:1-14 **The Time of Exile Foretold** For twenty three years Jeremiah foretold the fall of Judah v3. The first siege of Jerusalem occurred in 605 BC with deportation of people by Nebuchadnezzar including Daniel. In 604 BC eighteen years before the fall Jeremiah wrote in a book a prophecy that the time of captivity for the people would be seventy years v12,13. Babylon fell in 539 BC sixty five years after his prophecy and the first Jews returned to rebuild the Temple which was dedicated in 516 BC (586 to 516 BC).

25:15-38 **The Cup of God's Wrath** After judgment on God's people the surrounding nations would be judged. This reached finality under the Roman Empire around 63 BC.
In the last days the sin of all mankind will be judged – all nations and people will be required to give account v30-38; Rev 15:1.

26:1-24 **Perseverance** During the last twenty years before the fall of Jerusalem Jeremiah came under increased threat because of his unpopular message. As he foretold disaster and offered restoration the leaders became more hostile and he was threatened with death.

27:1-22 He warned the people to accept the yoke of Babylon and remain in their own land or they would be exiled. This resulted in more resistance, persecution and conflict.

28:1-17 Despite the positive words of the false prophets Jeremiah's prophecy was fulfilled.

29:1-32 **Good Citizens** After Jehoiachin was deported in 598 BC Jeremiah sent a letter to the exiles in Babylon telling them that it was God who exiled them and now gave them instructions to live by. They must accept this punishment for their sins - settle down and be good citizens v4,5. They should seek the peace and prosperity of the city and pray for it v7. They must not be deceived by false prophets and fortune tellers v8. **When the seventy years of exile were complete** God would bring them back to their homeland for he had plans to prosper them. They should call on him in prayer and seek him for he would be found when they sought him with all their hearts v 10-13. The people in exile followed this advice and within seventy years the Persians conquered Babylon allowing exiles to return no doubt influenced by their good citizenship. This message applies for us – God has plans to prosper us if we seek him with all our hearts and follow his requirements.

REDEMPTION

30:1-24 **Return From Exile** The people will return to their homeland. After being disciplined God will restore them to health, heal their wounds and restore their fortunes. The city of Jerusalem will be rebuilt. The survival, prosperity and continuity of the people of Israel in their own land since May 14, 1948 are testimony to the ongoing provision of God to this day.

The Time of Jacob's Trouble refers to **the awful day - none will be like it** v7; Zec 12:2-5. After it they will serve the LORD. This event will occur in the last days. The raising of a king like David looked forward to Jesus v9; Rev 16:16; 17:14.

31:1-40 **A New Covenant** Because of God's everlasting love v3 their mourning will turn to gladness, sorrow to joy v13. Repentance was foreseen v18,19. God will make a new Covenant with Israel - he will put his laws in their minds and hearts, forgive their wickedness and remember their sins no more v 31-34. The New Covenant established by Jesus was confirmed by the coming of the Holy Spirit Lk 22:19,20; Heb 8:6-13.

32:1-25 **Redemption assured** Jeremiah was imprisoned by Zedekiah for his message. Even as the army of Babylon besieged Jerusalem a word came to him to buy a local field indicating confidence that God would restore the people after the exile.

Ah, Sovereign LORD you have made the heavens and earth by your great power and outstretched arm - nothing is too hard for you v17. This is the confidence we have as we serve.

32:26-44 **The God of all Mankind** The everlasting Covenant in which the people will never turn away from him v40 is extended to people of all nations who respond to God and follow his ways. It was initiate by Jesus Mk 1:14,15.

33:1-13 Call to me and I will tell you great and unsearchable things you do not know v3 A further word came to Jeremiah in prison. Despite the devastation taking place people will be restored from captivity, healed, cleansed of sin and forgiven for their rebellion against God – when they call to him v6.

33:14-26 **The Righteous King** Again the long range prophecy was given of a righteous King from David's line and an eternal kingdom v15,22; 23:5,6. This will be fulfilled at the Second Coming of Jesus.

The Final Days of Jerusalem

34:1 to 36:32 In the midst of the siege Jeremiah again warned Zedekiah but without response so judgment was again pronounced. An earlier example of faithfulness came in the reign of Jehoiakim some twenty years before. At that time a family made a voluntary rule not to drink wine to which they had remained faithful. They were in contrast to the current people who were not faithful to God's Word. The judgment was sent on a scroll to Jehoiakim who burnt it. So another scroll was written and sent to the king.

37:1 to 38:28 **Imprisoned** Jeremiah was put in prison because of his consistent message of doom. The king wanted a good prophecy despite the evil that he had done and the enemy being at the gate. Jeremiah was threatened with death and lowered into a disused water cistern where he sank in the mud 38:6. Eventually he was returned to the courthouse until rescued by the Babylonians who learned of his prophecies 38:28. Despite all the evil he had done Zedekiah sent to Jeremiah for advice.

39:1-18 **Fall of Jerusalem** After a siege of eighteen months Jerusalem fell to the army of Babylon in 586 BC. Zedekiah deserted the city but was captured and taken into captivity along with many of the people – only the poor were left v10. Jeremiah was released from detention in the courthouse but later rounded up with the captives to be deported. The commander found him and released him to remain in Jerusalem. Jeremiah received a kind word for Ebed-Melech who had rescued him from the cistern.

40:1-16 **Gedaliah was appointed governor of Jerusalem** by Babylon and given charge over those who remained to live in peace v5. Many of those who escaped the Babylonians returned to the city to support Gedaliah.

41:1-18 **Assassination** Seven months later Gedaliah was assassinated by a traitor in league with the Ammorites and the surviving people fled towards Egypt fearing reprisal from Babylon. The corruption of the human heart is unpredictable!

42:1-22 **Flight into Egypt** They consulted Jeremiah for direction from the LORD which they committed to follow v5,6. They were told to remain in their homeland where God would protect them v10,11.

43:1-13 When told God's Word they once again disobeyed and headed for Egypt taking Jeremiah with them, against his will. As a result of his persecution and age of 70 years he was too frail to survive alone.

44:1-30 **The Fall of Egypt** The kings of Judah had sought protection from Egypt contrary to God's Word through Jeremiah. When Jerusalem fell those left still chose to go to Egypt where they adopted local gods. Jeremiah prophesied that Egypt too would fall v30 – eighteen years later Babylon conquered Egypt in 568 BC.

45:1-5 A prophetic word was given to Jeremiah's assistant and scribe Baruch for his faithful service.

Judgment on the Nations

46:1 to 49:39 **As God's judgment fell** on Israel and Judah he pronounced retribution on the surrounding nations who had been in conflict with his people and who took advantage of their weaknesses. God is sovereign over all nations and has concern for them. They included Egypt, Philistia, Moab, Ammon, Edom, Damascus (Syria), Kedar and Hazor (local tribes) and Elam (Persia) who would unite with Media to conquer Babylon in 539 BC.

50:1 to 51:64 **Nations of the World** Specific detail is given about the fall of Babylon which represents the united cities of the godless world Rev 18:1-24. The ultimate fulfilment of God's judgment will come in the last days when God's supreme reign is revealed with the return of the Lord Jesus Christ as King of kings and Lord of lords Rev 19:11-16. The words of Jeremiah end here! 51:64.

52:1-34 **Judah in Captivity** Further details were given of the fall of Jerusalem and the reasons for the captivity of the people of Judah.

A Message for Today Continued rejection of the Creator God and his right way to live will result in separation for eternity. Response to his goodness and mercy will result in eternity spent in his Presence. As in the days of Jeremiah, each of us has a choice 32:40.

Lamentations – 'mournful songs'

Introduction - As the message to honor God went unheeded the need for exile became clear. For twenty-three years under four evil kings Jeremiah faithfully foretold the fall of Jerusalem and warned the people not to trust in Egypt but to submit to Babylon for their own good as it was the discipline of the LORD. Had they submitted they could have remained in their homeland.
Jeremiah saw the outcome of his prophecies in the fall of Jerusalem and the exile of the people.
Author – Jeremiah, prophet of Judah.
Period – Around 586 BC following the destruction of Jerusalem.
Theme – What could have been if only we had listened Having warned the people of impending doom Jeremiah expressed his grief, sorrow and disappointment at the loss encountered by God's people in exile including the destruction of the Temple and city.

LESSONS TO BE LEARNED
1:1 to 5:22 We learn much from the lament of this great man about God and our approach to him (looked at in overview) -
• **Mourning** Sorrow and grief over the loss and what could have been 1:1. For all the physical glory of Israel in the time of the great kings David and Solomon there was a greater loss. The LORD had chosen Israel as his 'treasured possession' to be an example to the world Ex 19:5,6. He was their 'portion' 3:24 and they were his holy people. They had lost everything and were now captives in a foreign land again Ex 2:23
• **Consequence of Sin** The sins of the people were the cause of suffering 1:8,14. The people were misled because the teachers and prophets did not speak the truth 2:14. We cannot complain when we suffer justly 3:39. The prophets and priests had failed morally 4:13
• **God's Righteous Judgment** God is just in all things 1:18. They had been warned repeatedly and refused to respond 2:17
• **Repentance and Confession** Repentance requires sorrow 2:18,19. We must examine our ways and come into agreement with God about the offence of sin 3:40. We must acknowledge our sins and confess them to God 3:41,42
• **Return to the LORD** Repentance must be followed by action – turning away from the old ways and turning to the LORD 5:21

- **Hope for the future** There is hope for future restoration – because of the LORD's great love we are not consumed, for his compassions never fail. We must call this to mind - it is our basis for hope 3:21,22.
- **They are new every morning** - great is God's faithfulness 3:23 We should acknowledge his blessings every morning and at all times!
- **The LORD is good to those who hope in him** who seek him. It is good to wait quietly for the salvation of the LORD 3:25,26. God is not vindictive – discipline is for our good 3:31-33
- **A Faithful Servant** Over forty-five years of persecution and rejection, despite the odds against him, with little evidence of response from the people Jeremiah never lost his faith and remained faithful to his calling from God. He continued with God's message 3:40-42 and retained his dependence on God 3:55-60. He is a great example to us not to give up witnessing to Jesus and doing what God calls us to do
- **Call for Mercy** We must always appeal to the favor of God and depend on him in all things – it is by his goodness and grace that we have all things, from birth to the grave and beyond 5:1
- **The Sovereignty of God** The LORD reigns forever 5:19. He is in control of all things – calamities and good things to come 3:37,38; Is 54:16,17.

Failure of the Monarchy Israel had reached its lowest point in history. After five hundred years of kings they had shown that there is a need for a new kingdom with a perfect ruler – prophet, priest and king. The prophetic books of the Old Testament foretold the coming of a king. These messianic prophecies were fulfilled in the appearing of Jesus Christ Jn 4:25,26.

Implications for Today Jeremiah's prophecies and lamentations are relevant in godless, materialistic, self-centered societies today - especially those who have the message of the God of love and his plan of salvation through Jesus Christ.

All the promises of God to Abraham still apply 2Cor 1:20; Gal 3:29 Israel as a nation failed to remain faithful to God and his commandments. They also did not take God's eternal plan of salvation to the people of the world. The new Messiah would establish the eternal kingdom to embrace believing people of all nations Rev 5:9,10. That message and kingdom continue to spread around the world today.

Ezekiel – 'God is strong'

Introduction – Born in 623 BC Ezekiel grew up in Jerusalem and was taken into captivity in 597 BC at the age of 26. He lived among the people in exile and was commissioned by God to be a prophet seven years before the fall of Jerusalem in 586 BC continuing till fifteen years after the fall, a total of 22 years 40:1. A contemporary of Daniel they had no direct contact.

Author - Ezekiel, priest and prophet among the exiles in Babylon from 593–571 BC.

Period – The Assyrian empire dominated the Fertile Crescent from 885 BC. In 612 BC Assyria fell to Babylon under Nabopolassar 626-605 BC who died shortly after leaving his son Nebuchadnezzar as king 605-562 BC. Judah took the opportunity to rebel against the new authority.

In 605 BC Nebuchadnezzar besieged Jerusalem 2Kin 24:1; 2Chr 36:6. He entered the city and took tribune from Jehoiakim, king of Judah. The royal family and nobility including Daniel were exiled to Babylon.

In 597 BC Nebuchadnezzar lay siege to Jerusalem for the second time 2 Kin 24:10-14; 2Chr 36:9,10 deporting Jehoiachin, king of Judah to Babylon along with 10,000 officials, leaders and skilled people including Ezekiel. After continued revolt Jerusalem and the Temple were finally destroyed by Nebuchadnezzar in 586 BC.

Theme – **The people in exile** expected that they would soon return to Jerusalem. Ezekiel spoke against the false prophets who promoted this view. He warned the people of God's inevitable judgment on sin, the importance of individual responsibility and the need for a personal relationship with God.

Restoration After the fall of Jerusalem he foretold the repentance and restoration of Israel as a unified nation.

The Messiah He also foresaw end time events – the coming of a righteous king and a millennium kingdom 21:27; 37:24-28.

The Sovereign LORD The frequent use of this title helps us in our relationship with God as we recognize the dominion of God over the people and nations of the earth and over our individual situations as well 4:14; 5:5; 36:23; 37:3.

A Vision of the Glory of God

1:1-28 **The Presence of God** Exiled in 597 BC Ezekiel became a priest in exile in 587 BC (at 30 years of age). Among the exiles in

Babylon he received a vision and commission to be a prophet in 593 BC v2.

Four living creatures representing created beings – man, lion, ox and eagle v5. We expect that this revelation of God to Ezekiel would compare with the later revelation to John Rev 4:6-8 -

• *Wings, wheels v11,15,16* – representing mobility, motion. God is omnipresent - present in all places

• *Flashes of lightning v14* - power, activity. God is omnipotent - the source of all energy Gen 1:34; Rev 4:5; 8:3-5

• *Full of eyes* – nothing is hidden from his knowledge. God is omniscient, all seeing v18; Heb 4:12,13

• *Above the expanse – a throne – a figure like that of a man v26.* God may be represented symbolically in human terms (anthropomorphism). However God is Spirit – without physical form Jn 4:24.

This was the appearance of the likeness of the glory of the LORD v28 As with Moses, Ezekiel only saw the glory of God Ex 33:20–23.

I fell face down – the reverent response of all who experience the personal glory of God v28 - Abraham, Moses, Isaiah, Jeremiah.

The Call to be a Prophet of God

2:1 Son of Man This unique title given to Ezekiel was chosen by Jesus the **Son of God** to emphasize that he had taken on manhood in order to save mankind Jn 3:14. It also identified him with the Messiah Dan 7:13,14.

2:2 **In the Spirit** Ezekiel felt the hand of the LORD 1:3, heard the voice of the LORD v1, encountered the Spirit of the LORD v2; 3:14 - we have the Holy Spirit within and must learn to respond to his leading Jn 14:17; Rev 1:9-11.

2:3-10 **I am sending you to the Israelites** All that remained of the original nation of twelve tribes of Israel were Judah, Benjamin, the Levites and the remnants of the other tribes who remanded in Jerusalem because of the Temple worship. The northern tribes were dispersed by Assyria with the fall of Samaria in 722 BC. The term Israel referred to what remained of the chosen people. They were *a rebellious nation – obstinate and stubborn v3,4.*

You must speak my words whether they listen or not – the task of a prophet and of a witness v7. We are also asked to suffer in order to carry out God's will and we can be sure God will equip us for the task Lk 9:26.

The Message of Judgment

3:1-11 A Scroll to be eaten – it is sweet to share the Word of God v3. We must meditate on it till it becomes fire in our bellies Jer 20:9.

They are not willing to listen to me – the great sin of mankind is to deny the existence and authority of God v7.

3:12-15 Encounter with God Ezekiel was overwhelmed by the vision and encounter with God v15.

3:16-27 Responsibilities of a Watchman We must warn people of impending doom v18. Each individual is accountable to God for their own response to the revelation of God v19; 33:1-20. The vision was repeated to prepare Ezekiel for the task.

The Fall of Jerusalem Predicted

4:1-17 The city would come under siege (previous sieges occurred in 605 and 597 BC) v2. Ezekiel was required to demonstrate symbols of the siege –

- he made a clay map of the city and built siege walls and battering-rams
- he held an iron pan to show that God would turn his face from the city
- he lay on his left side for 390 days and on his right side for 40 days tied with rope and only starvation rations – to show the magnitude of the sins of the people - one day for each year v5. Israel bore their sin from Solomon to the return from exile (930 - 539 BC = 390 years). Judah was assigned 40 years, one generation v6. Famine occurred in the final siege v16,17.

5:1-17 Ezekiel shaved his head (a shame) and used the hair to show the fate of the people – destroyed with the city, slaughtered in the attack or exiled.

This would be in response to Judah's wickedness and rebellion against God's laws. Even with Jerusalem under tribute and many of the people already in exile there was no change of conduct v6. *You have not even conformed to the standards of the nations around you v7;* Rom 12:1,2. *I will make you a ruin and a reproach among the nations v14* – this was fulfilled in 586 BC and continued until 1948 when Israel again became an official state.

6:1-14 God was grieved by adulterous hearts that turn away from him. We cannot appreciate the offense of sin to God.

7:1-27 They would be dealt with according to their conduct and standards. If we reject God's offer of salvation how can we object to his response 6:10.

8:1-18 Idolatry was committed in the Temple – other man made gods with and before the LORD.

9:1-11 All who had not offended were identified and would be spared. God always differentiates his people Ex 8:32

The Glory of the LORD departed from the Temple

10:1-22 A vision of the glory of God in the Temple was revealed v4. The glory of God then departed v18,19. We have the privilege of knowing God's Presence and must pursue it in our daily lives Eph 4:30; 1Thes 5:19. The consequence of continued sin and rejection of God is the loss of the Presence of God both now and for eternity v18. The glory then left the city 11:23.

Retribution and Restoration

11:1-25 Punishment of the leaders and people would be followed by a new period when Israel would be restored with a new heart and spirit v19.

12:1-28 Ezekiel enacted the exile of the inhabitants of Jerusalem in an effort to obtain their response but to no avail.

13:1-23 The worldly prophets and idolaters who taught and practiced evil would be cut off for leading the people astray.

14:1-23 Judgment was unavoidable. Daniel is included by Ezekiel with Noah and Job as righteous v14.

15:1-8 Jerusalem was a useless vine – producing nothing good.

16:1-63 Israel was an adopted child, an adulterous wife, who returned to the ways of the heathen past. An everlasting covenant will be made providing atonement for sin v60,63.

17:1-24 God planted Israel like a shoot but when it grew it turned to Babylon. So he will take another shoot and it will flourish – birds of every kind will nest in it v22,23. This shoot is the kingdom of heaven proclaimed by Jesus Mt 13:31-35. God determines the progress and outcome of all things v24.

Individual Responsibility and God's Mercy

18:1-22 Every Living Soul Belongs to Me - the soul who sins is the one who will die v4 These truths must be recognized by every individual person. The consequence of sin cannot be avoided – *all have sinned and come short of the glory of God - the penalty for sin is death Rom 3:23; 6:23.*

18:23-32 Do I take any pleasure of the death of the wicked? declares the Sovereign LORD. Rather, am I not pleased when they turn from their ways and live? God's grace is confirmed in the New Covenant - *he is patient with you, not wanting anyone to perish, but everyone to come to repentance 2Pet 3:9.* A new heart and new spirit are given to those who accept Jesus as Savior Jn 1:12. Hell is a destination of choice Mt 25:41.

19:1-14 The downfall of Israel's leaders was lamented.

20:1-29 I gave them my decrees and made known to them my laws, for the man who obeys them will live by them v11 The Ten Commandments came through Israel and became the foundation of western civilization. They are the basis for the moral code of our society and the wellbeing of all people.

20:30-49 **God's Plan for His People** - *I will show myself holy among you in the sight of the nations* - God's intention is always to bless his people and reveal himself as holy to the nations of the world through them v41.

21:1-23 Babylon will be God's sword of judgment – Jerusalem fell after a two year siege.

21:24-27 **The kingdom of Israel will be lost** - ruined until the **throne is restored to the rightful king** v27. This will be fulfilled at the Second Coming of Jesus Gen 49:10; Lk 1:31-33; Rom 11:25-32.

21:28-32 Ammon, enemy of Judah to the east of Jordan also fell to Babylon 586 AD.

22:1-31 **The Need to Pray and Witness** No one had regard for God or for the moral decline of the people. Bad things happen when good people do nothing. *I looked for a man among them who would build up the wall and stand before me in the gap on behalf of the land so I would not have to destroy it but I found none v30* – this statement by God encourages us to be faithful in praying for our families, leaders and nation and in witnessing to them 1Tim 2:1-8. In God's economy the prayers of 'one man' can turn the tide! v23; Jas 5:16-18.

23:1-49 **Adulterous People** Israel and Judah were portrayed as two adulterous sisters. They belonged to God – he created them, chose them, redeemed them out of Egypt and delivered them into the Promised Land. All he required was their affection, loyalty and obedience to his just ways, for their own good. But they gave themselves to others. So he gave them over to discipline.

God's actions are never vindictive but measured by justice.

The Siege and Fall of Jerusalem

24:1-14 Ezekiel was told the day of the start of the third siege in 588 BC v1,2. It became like a cooking pot. Two years later the city fell.

24:15-27 He was required to foretell the death of his wife but not to mourn as an example of the pain to God at the loss of the sanctuary and the coming pain the people would suffer because of their sin.

Judgment on the surrounding Nations Is 13:1 to 23:18

25:1-17 Because Israel's neighbors were antagonistic to Judah they too would come under God's judgment - Ammon, Moab, Edom and Philistia all benefited from the fall of Jerusalem and fell to Babylon after 586 BC.

26:1 to 27:36 Tyre and Sidon took advantage of the fall of Jerusalem as were also destroyed by Babylon 575 BC.

28:1-26 **Pride and arrogance** Tyre can be seen as symbolic of the pride and fall of Satan 28:11-19; Is 14:12-15.

29:1 to 32:32 Egypt was conquered by Cambyses, son of Cyrus and was under Persian rule 525-40 BC.

33:1-20 **A Watchman** Ezekiel's appointment to warn of the destruction of Jerusalem was due to the mercy of God in giving the people a final chance to repent of their rebellion and sin. As believers we are called to tell others about Jesus. God wants all people to turn to him v11; 18:23.

33:21-33 **Fall of Jerusalem** After two years of siege Jerusalem finally fell in 586 BC as predicted. Ezekiel was advised by an escapee v21.

A New Shepherd

34:1-10 **The Shepherds and the Sheep** The shepherds were the nobility, leaders and priests who received their positions from God to exercise direction and care for the people. God spoke against them because they had not fulfilled their duty to the people. This role is given to government, community and church leaders today. The same judgment will come against leaders in the nations who fail their responsibilities v4.

34:11-24 **The Good Shepherd -** *I myself will search for my sheep and look after them v11.* This word was fulfilled when Jesus the Good Shepherd came to save the lost and make available eternal life - *my sheep listen to my voice; I know them and they follow me. I give them eternal life* Jn 10:11-16; 27-30. *I will place over them one shepherd v23;* Jn 21:17. Again Jesus used a prophetic title to identify his appointment as Messiah.

***34:25-31* A New Covenant** This will involve a covenant of peace, safety and showers of blessing v25.

35:1-15 Edom in the south, descendants of Esau and Abraham and hostile to Judah and Israel will be laid waste.

Restoration of God's People

Ezekiel's prophecies now concerned the future restoration of God's people.

***36:1-23* The Glory of God will be Revealed** *The nations will know that I am the LORD - when I show myself holy through you before their eyes v23.* This is the responsibility of the believer – God will show that he is holy through us. How many in the church through the ages have failed to carry out this assignment? May we give our best effort to be faithful as royal priests in our generation Mt 5:16; 1Pet 2:9.

***36:24-38* The New Covenant Confirmed** The promise of restoration has reference to a new kingdom with renewed people – with new hearts and the indwelling presence of the Holy Spirit v26-28.

***37:1-13* The valley of dry bones** being commanded to rise represents the restoration of God's people Israel and Judah. They will be raised by the breath of God, an outpouring of the Holy Spirit v4-6.

This began physically with the re-establishment of Israel as a nation in May 14, 1948. Israel will be the scene of major conflict in the last days leading to the coming of Jesus.

***37:15-28* One Nation and One King** Israel will be united under one nation and one Messianic king - a prophecy to be fulfilled by Jesus. He will be of the line of David v24,25; 2Sam 7:16. This prophecy tells of the millennium reign and the eternal kingdom to follow v26-28.

***38:1-23* End Time Rebellion** In the last days godless nations of the world will unite - represented by Gog and Magog in the north, Meshech and Tubal in Asia Minor, Persia in the east, Cush and Put in the south, Gomer and Togarmah, also in Turkey - *you and all your troops and many nations with you v9.* This includes the surrounding nations and nations to the north hostile to Israel today. Israel is identified as gathered and living in safety v8. They will invade Israel as a combined act of defiance against God Rev 17:12-14. The purpose of this conflict will be to further establish the rebellious nature of mankind and make known the sovereignty of God - *so that the nations may know when I show myself holy through you before their eyes v16.*

They will be defeated by the hand of God. A great earthquake will destroy their cities v19; Rev 16:18-21.

39:1-24 The aftermath of this conflict shows the magnitude of the victory - it will be absolute v1-25.

39:24-29 **The Millennium Rule** Those remaining nations not involved in the northern invasion will be united under the antichrist Rev 17:12-14. This final stand of the kingdoms of the world against God and his people will be defeated by the return of Jesus, the King of kings Rev 19:11-21. This will lead to the millennium reign on earth with all nations subject to him Zec 14:1-21; Rev 20:4-6.

The New Temple - the City of God

40:1 to 46:24 **The Final Vision** came in 572 BC. As with other visions this was a real experience reported by Ezekiel – not an imaginary picture of his own making v2. Ezekiel was born into a priestly family and saw the vision of the future in terms of the restoration of the Temple, the Temple services and the Old Covenant blessings. His vision did not conform to the details of other Temple dimensions but looked forward to the time when the New City will be established and God will dwell with his people forever Zec 6:9-15; Rev 21:1-5 (ref p96).

47:1-12 **The River from the Temple** This foretold the presence of the Holy Spirit and the abundance of eternal life which we experience through faith in Jesus as a foretaste of the coming City of God Jn 7:37-39; 10:10; Rev 22:1,2.

48:35 The name of the city from that time on will be THE LORD IS THERE. This is confirmed in the New Testament – *The throne of God and of the Lamb will be in the city and his servants will serve him there Rev 22:3.*

The New Kingdom The second Temple begun by Herod in 19 BC and destroyed by the Roman general Titus in 70 AD showed there had been no change in the hearts and behavior of mankind. A New Covenant and kingdom was required as prophesied by Ezekiel 36:24-27. This was established by Jesus and will be fulfilled at his Second Coming.

Daniel – God is my Judge

Introduction – Born in Jerusalem around 620 BC and taken to Babylon in exile in 605 BC as a youth Daniel was a contemporary of Ezekiel born around 623 BC. As a noble he became a Hebrew statesman in the court of Babylon dealing with heathen kings rather than a priest or prophet among the people of Israel as was the case with Ezekiel. Daniel gained favor before five foreign kings over a period of some fifty-seven years due to his loyalty to God. Though not commissioned as a prophet he received extraordinary prophetic ability. He lived to around 87 years of age.

The Books of Ezra and Nehemiah record the return of the remnant of Judah to Jerusalem. Cyrus II, the Great, king of Persia (559-530 BC) conquered Babylon in 539 BC as foretold Is 21:2,9; 44:24-28. Judah had been in captivity for almost seventy years as foretold by Jeremiah Jer 25:12. This was interpreted by Daniel from Scripture and led to his prayer for fulfilment 9:2. The decree was given in 538 BC Ezr 1:1. Many decided to return to their homeland to rebuild the Temple and revive the worship and keeping of the Law.

The first six chapters tell of Daniel's experience in the foreign court – the last six describe his revelations of future events.

Some have criticized the Book of Daniel because it is hard to accept the accuracy and details of his amazing prophecies. We may have confidence in the historical and archeological verification of the sixth century authorship of the book. Daniel revealed detailed knowledge of the period. It is consistent with Ezra, Nehemiah and Esther and of what is now known of the Babylonian and Persian periods at the time of the Exile (ref Ezra Introduction).

The Book of Daniel was included in the listing of the 'Prophetic Books' of the Old Testament Canon (prior to AD 400). It was transferred to the 'Writings' (history) because although Daniel had the gift of prophecy he did not have the office. Daniel was confirmed as a prophet by Jesus Mt 24:15.

Author – Daniel, statesman and prophet in exile 605-533 BC.

Period – In 605 BC Nebuchadnezzar first besieged Jerusalem 2Kin 24:1; 2Chr 36:6. Some of the royal family and nobility including Daniel were exiled to Babylon. In 586 BC after continued revolt Jerusalem and the Temple were finally destroyed by Nebuchadnezzar. The exiles were permitted to return under Cyrus II in 538 BC.

Daniel the person - Of noble birth he was trained in the learning and ways of the Babylonian court. He was faithful, obedient, highly favored by God and identified as a righteous man Ezk 14:14. Above all he was a man of the Word of God and prayer 9:2,3. A Jewish exile of exemplary character, a person of integrity with significant leadership ability he established a relationship with and the respect of five foreign kings, even the sacrilegious Belshazzer. Because of the quality of his life God chose to give him a message for all ages – including dreams, long term prophecies and foretelling the coming of the Messiah. He was separated from the wizards of Babylon and Persia and put in charge of them because of his prophetic abilities but was not involved in their practices. It is impossible to remove the miracles, prophecies, dreams and visions and the period from the record of Daniel.

Theme - God is sovereign over the nations of the world and is inexorably working his purposes out His plan for his chosen people (Abraham, Moses, judges, kings) continued with their return to the world stage in time for the coming of the Messiah. God preserved a remnant, according to his Covenant - otherwise they would have been absorbed among the nations.

The prophecies were given as the people returned to the desolation of Jerusalem so they would know the future is in God's hand and be encouraged to hold their faith. They related to world history leading up to the Messiah and the destruction of the Temple in AD 70. They applied to foreign kings and the Jewish people. They were not for Daniel's time alone 8:26; 12:4,9. Many were fulfilled over the next 570 years of history in the rise and fall of the kingdoms of Babylon, Persia, Greece and Rome. Some are still to be fulfilled.

Messiah and the Eternal Kingdom Daniel foretold the coming of the Messiah Jesus Christ and the eternal kingdom in the end time.

God's faithfulness is demonstrated to those who put their trust in him in all generations, even in exile. The events show there is no situation in which God cannot protect his own - not a fiery furnace nor a lions den. When we are fully convinced of God's sovereign power with us in all things we can move into the future without fear.

SUMMARY
Daniel Established in the Court of Babylon 1:1-21
The Eternal Kingdom of the Messiah 2:1-49

DANIEL ESTABLISHED IN THE COURT OF BABYLON

1:1-21 **Jerusalem was besieged three times by Babylon** The first time was in 605 BC. The Temple was raided and tribute extracted – vessels taken from the Temple feature in the last feast in Babylon 5:2. It was common practice to take captives from the nobility to train and use in the king's service v3. Daniel and his three companions refused to eat food offered to an idol v8. God gives favor to his servants even in the midst of the enemy v9. The reward for faithfulness is blessing in all areas of one's life v17.

Daniel served in the Babylonian court till it fell in 539 BC and beyond v21. The new kingdom of Babylon had only survived as a world power for some 70 years to carry out God's judgment on Judah (612-539 BC) Jer 25:9,11,12.

THE ETERNAL KINGDOM OF THE MESSIAH

2:1-28 **Nebuchadnezzar had a dream** 603 BC. As a test he required his advisers to tell him the dream as well as the interpretation which they could not do. When told of the consequences Daniel and his friends turned to prayer – God answered by revealing the dream and Daniel gave praise v18–23.

He changes times and seasons: he sets up kings and deposes them v20,21. This is the authority by which we pray for our situations, our leaders and nations. Daniel acknowledged God as the source of his knowledge – *there is a God in heaven who reveals mysteries v28.*

2:29-43 **Kingdoms to Come** The interpretation of the dream was given to the king. It foretold future events and four great kingdoms.

A statue symbolic of world dominance -
* the gold represented Babylon 612 BC already present as a world empire and soon to fall v32
* the silver represented Medo-Persia with two arms soon to be united in 549 BC under Cyrus II king of Persia who then conquered Babylon 539 BC
* the bronze represented Greece who conquered Persia 332 BC
* the iron represented pagan Rome which succeeded Greece 63 BC with two legs (West and East - Rome and Byzantium!). Rome was overrun by the Goths AD 476 and Constantinople was conquered by the Turks (Muslims) AD 1453 v33,40; 7:23
* the feet of iron and clay represent ten kings of the end time v33,41;7:24; Rev 17:3,12.

This prophecy was given at the height of the power of the Babylonian Empire. Recorded in 603 BC it accurately foresaw the rise and fall of Babylon, Persia, Greece and Rome. It was included in the Greek translation of the Hebrew Old Testament (Septuagint LXX) in 275-250 BC during Greek domination of Mesopotamia and predating the rise of Rome v31-34.

2:44-49 The Eternal Kingdom As the point of the dream a rock was cut out, but not by human hands - by the hand of God! It struck the statue on its feet, smashed the kingdoms of the world like chaff and swept them away without trace v34,35.

This rock is the eternal kingdom of God It was established by Jesus Christ the Messiah during the rule of Rome as a result of his death and resurrection and is open to all who will enter it. It was set up, as foretold *in the time of those kings - never to be destroyed! v44.*

It will crush all those kingdoms and bring them to an end but it will itself endure forever v44 - it will replace all the kingdoms of the world - to be fulfilled in the end time Rev 11:15.

The import and accuracy of the predictions of this dream concerning the future world empires has caused skeptics to doubt the veracity of the Book of Daniel. The accuracy of the prophecies gives added assurance of the certainty of the Eternal Kingdom of God.

Why did God reveal the future to this heathen imperial king at the height of power? Babylon came to power around 610 BC and had just conquered Jerusalem. God made it known that after a series of 'known world' empires there will be a time of accountability for all mankind and his eternal kingdom will ultimately triumph over the kingdoms of the world Rev 12:10.

This dream and interpretation were also given at this time to encourage God's people that, even though they were being disciplined the future is in God's hand and all things will work ultimately for their good.

The statue represented the kingdoms of the world from the point of view of mankind.

2:46-49 **The King's Response** Daniel was given a place of honor and authority. This is understandable as Daniel had passed the king's test v5.

A TEST OF FAITH – the fiery furnace

3:1-30 An enormous image was built perhaps in response to the dream - 27 meters high. All were required to worship it on pain of death – this will be an end time event Rev 13:14-18.

The God we serve is able to save us v16-18 Daniel's three friends refused and were thrown into the furnace. They were confident God could deliver them and even if he chose not to they would honor him – an example for us.

A fourth man was there – God will not only deliver us but be with us in all situations when we trust him v25. The king promoted the three men v28-30.

This event occurred to demonstrate that God's people will not bow down to the images of the world. May we have the courage to stand in the face of persecution confident that our times are in the hand of the LORD Ps 31:15-17.

A LESSON IN HUMILITY

4:1-37 Nebuchadnezzar had another dream which only Daniel could interpret v8. The dream was a warning from God that the king's pride and ruthless ways were up for judgment v19.

So that the living may know that the Most High is sovereign over the kingdoms of men and gives them to anyone he wishes v17 We may not understand situations around the world but we can be sure that the LORD is in control. He was about to intervene in the life of Nebuchadnezzar. Again we see the authority with which we come before God in prayer 2:21.

Renounce your sins by doing what is right and your wickedness by being kind to the oppressed v27 The sickness to Nebuchadnezzar is actually recorded in history (a temporary mental disorder) v30-34. Even foreign kings will be humbled by God to suit his purposes v34-37. These dramatic events brought understandable response from the king resulting in him acknowledging God 2:46; 4:34-37. Our prayers and witness will also produce results.

THE FALL OF BABYLON – the writing on the wall

5:1-31 This event occurred sixty years later 539 BC. Belshazzar was co-regent - second highest ruler in the kingdom with his father Nabonidus (sometime absent) v7. He gave a banquet and desecrated the vessels from the Temple in Jerusalem 2Kin 24:13. A hand appeared and wrote four words which terrified Belshazzar and which only Daniel could interpret v5-17 - 'God has numbered your days – you have been weighed and found wanting - your kingdom is divided and given to the Medes and Persians' v25-28.

That very night – the army of **Cyrus II** king of the newly unified Medo-Persian Empire conquered Babylon v30. History records that Cyrus diverted the river Euphrates so that the impregnable city could be entered without resistance. **Daruis, a Mede** and aging noble was made governor over the city while Cyrus continued his conquest v31. Nabonidus returned but was defeated.

AN EXCEPTIONAL CHARACTER – the lion's den

6:1-28 Daniel became a leader in the new administration under Persian rule. He was now eighty-one years old. The other leaders sought to undermine his position but *could find no corruption in him because he was trustworthy and neither corrupt nor negligent - we will never find any basis for charges against this man Daniel unless it has something to do with the law of his God v4,5*. It must be our aim to be without offence before God and man.

When Daniel learned of the plot (requiring prayer only to the king) he continued his devotion to pray three times a day to God v10. He was put into the den of lions but was protected from harm v21. The evil plan against Daniel was turned to his favor by God v26. So he continued to prosper in the reigns of Darius and Cyrus II (possibly for the last four years of his life).

Daniel encountered the den of lions to show that God's people will be loyal in all circumstances and faithful in prayer.

REVELATIONS OF THE FUTURE

Daniel personally received a series of dreams and visions after he was seventy years of age. God revealed prophetic truths about the future kingdoms of the world and the coming eternal kingdom of Jesus Christ. As with the earlier interpretations Daniel's visions were direct revelations from God 7:1.

Why did God give these messages at this time? God's people were returning from exile and they needed to know the next stage of their history. This required the rebuilding of Jerusalem and re-establishing the Temple worship in preparation for the coming of the Messiah promised by the prophets and the New Covenant Is 42:1-9; Rev 14:1-5.

REVELATION 1 – End Time Judgment of the Nations

7:1-8 **Four Warring Beasts** – Daniel received a vision in 553 BC. As Nebuchadnezzar had been given the human view of the world's kingdoms 2:31, Daniel received a view from God's perspective – they are like warring beasts.

The four winds of heaven indicate the importance of this message for all mankind v2. The interpretation received fifty years after Nebuchadnezzar's dream provided further detail particularly about the end time 2:29-43 -

• a lion with wings of an eagle representing Babylon v4 - the change in nature and the new heart depicting the king's acknowledgment of God 4:34 - then

• a bear raised on one side representing Medo-Persia v5 who conquered Babylon 539 BC and Egypt 525 BC and attacked Athens 490 BC (the three ribs) - then

• a leopard with wings like a bird and four heads representing Greece and

• a fourth beast *terrifying and frightening - different from all the former beasts*, with iron teeth - symbolizing Rome (the most dominant empire to date - a superpower) but even more evil v7.

These four beasts compare with the statue in the dream of Nebuchadnezzar - the head of gold, chest of silver, belly and thighs of bronze and the legs and feet of iron and clay - representing world empires 2:32,33; 40-43.

• ten horns representing kings will arise from the final 'fourth' kingdom v7.20,24 – compare with 2:33,34

• another **'little horn'** (an eleventh horn) will come up among them - with a mouth that spoke boastfully v8 – to be destroyed in the end time v26.

7:9-14 **The Ancient of Days Holds Court** At this time the Eternal God set up thrones in court – books were opened and judgment was carried out -

There before me was one like a son of man coming in the clouds of heaven - He was given authority, glory and sovereign power, all peoples nations and men of every language worshipped him. His dominion is an everlasting dominion that will not pass away and his kingdom is one that will never be destroyed v13,14; Rev 20:12-15.

Ancient of Days v9 - symbolic reference to the Most High God because of his eternal being – a description also associated with Jesus Mic 5:2; Rev 1:14.

Son of man v13 - refers to 'the likeness of man' and was used frequently by God to address Ezekiel. It was also used in a special sense by Daniel to refer to this vision of the Messiah. Jesus took the title to refer to himself – no one else referred to him in this way – it is recorded eighty times in the Gospels Mt 8:20; 16:27,28. It emphasizes his divine and human nature.

The Most High God gave authority to the **Son of Man** - his dominion is everlasting and his kingdom eternal v13,14; Mt 28:18; Rev 5:12; 19:16.

7:15-18 **End Time Conflict** More detail was then given of the last days leading up to the Second Coming of Jesus. The first three beasts (kingdoms) were quickly dismissed to focus on the fourth beast and the 'little horn' v8.

7:19-25 **The Little Horn** The fourth Kingdom, while symbolic of the Roman Empire 2:40, will be **a world kingdom of the last days**, combining all the evil of previous kingdoms. Ten kings will rise from this kingdom for a short period. An eleventh king, the little horn, will wage war against the saints defeating them until God pronounces judgment and the saints possess the kingdom Rev 17:12.

He speaks against God and is thrown into the lake of fire v11; Rev 19:20. The little horn is the antichrist of the end time and identifies with **the dragon and two beasts** of Revelation Rev 12:3; 13:1,11 representing the devil and the final world empire - centralized governance and ideology, that will appear in the end time v21,22.

The beast out of the sea Rev 13:2 symbolizes the final world empire and has the combined likeness of a leopard, bear and lion incorporating all the evil features of previous empires v4-6. This end time ruler will have ten horns and seven heads (ten toes that were smashed 2:34) Rev 13:1. He is also given a mouth to utter proud words and blasphemies v11; Rev

13:5,6. He is given power to make war against the saints and to conquer them v21; Rev 13:7. He equates with the little horn of Daniel.

7:26-28 In Summary There will be increased persecution of faithful believers by godless society. A confederacy of ten kings will arise out of the ultimate world empire worse than all that went before. A further king - this **little horn** will appear as the antichrist - the personification of evil v23-25; Rev 13:2 who will devour the whole earth v23; Rev 13:7 and will be overthrown by the King of kings at his return v26,27; Rev 19:11-20. The time will come when the saints receive and possess the kingdom forever v18,27; Rev 21:3.

The essential message of this vision is that as the kingdoms of the world continue to deteriorate and come together in rebellion against God and his people there will be a day of judgment when all will be held accountable.

REVELATION 2 – Temple Desolation – received 551 BC

8:1-27 A Ram and a Goat This vision was of particular application for Daniel's people in exile. The symbols were clearly identified v20-22. Babylon is not mentioned (although 12 years remained under their rule) -
• the ram with two horns represented the Medes and Persians v20 (two kingdoms that were being united under Cyrus II at the very time of this prophecy 550 BC)
• the goat with the large horn represented Greece under Alexander who was to conquer Persia and the known world in eight years from 332 BC v21
• his empire was divided into four kingdoms after his death (the broken horn) which were ruled by four generals (representing the four prominent horns) - they were Ptolemy in Egypt, Seleucus in Syria, Cassander in Macedonia and Lysimachus in Thrace v22.
• out of one of them another horn, a stern faced king would rise v9, v23. This **other horn** is a forerunner of the end time **little horn** (eleventh horn) of the first vision 7:8. The desecration of the Temple by this other horn v9 amazingly occurred under Antiochus Epiphanes, the eighth Seleucid ruler in Syria in 167 BC when he invaded the 'Beautiful Land' v9. He desecrated the Temple and prevented Levitical sacrifices in an attempt to destroy Jewish faith. The Temple was not cleansed till 164 BC - *for 2300 evenings and mornings v24;* 9:26,27.

However this was only a foretaste of the future - it also concerned the time of the end v17-19,26; Mt; 24:15. This other horn prefigures the little horn of the end time - the antichrist. The desecration was a symbol of the rising force of evil marshalling against God and his people to be revealed as the ultimate antichrist of the last days v17; Rev 13:1-10.

REVELATION 3 – The Seventy Years of Exile – received 539 BC

9:1,2 Daniel understood from the Scriptures according to the Word of the LORD given to Jeremiah that the desolation of Jerusalem would last seventy years Jer 25:11-13; 29:10; 2Chr 36:21. From his study of the Word of God, the writings of Jeremiah, Daniel recognized that the seventy years prophesied for the time of the captivity, the Sabbath rest Lev 26:33,34, was almost up. He had been in exile for 67 years (605 – 538 BC). Jerusalem had been destroyed for 48 years since 586 BC.

9:3 So I turned to the LORD God and pleaded with him in prayer, petition, fasting and in sackcloth and ashes This shows the way in which God uses his people in order to accomplish his preordained purposes Ezk 22:30.

9:4-19 Daniel's prayer is a model for us -
• he recognized God's greatness and righteousness v4,7,14,16
• he confirmed the reason for the suffering of the people was due to their sin and rebellion from God v5
• he confessed the sins on behalf of the people v5,6,9-11
• he asked God to restore the Temple and forgive the people v17-19
• his request was based on God's mercy and on his Word v17-19; Jer 29:10.

9:20-23 **Believing Prayer** *As soon as you began to pray an answer was given v23* God had already provided for the return of his people with the conquest of Babylon by Persia. The answer was granted immediately but delayed due to the evil one 10:12-14. We must always persevere in prayer until we see the result Jas 1:6,7.

Persevering Prayer Here we see the reason for perseverance. Jesus taught that we must never give up in prayer Lk 18:1. Many do not receive answer to prayer because they do not have faith to continue Lk 18:8. A person who gives up must not expect answer to prayer because they are 'double minded' Jas 1:6-8. Persistent prayer is powerful and effective Jas 5:16.

Notice - Daniel was *highly esteemed* in the Presence of God v23.

Prophecy fulfilled The prophet Isaiah had already foretold the exile of Judah and that in addition Cyrus II, the Great, king of Persia would release the future Jewish exiles from Babylon to rebuild Jerusalem and the Temple Is 44:24-28. These events would have seemed incredible at the time of the prophecy (before 690 BC) but occurred over 150 years later Ezr 1:1-4.

When Cyrus 559-530 BC conquered Babylon in 539 BC Darius the Mede, was made governor, while Cyrus continued his conquests 11:1. Daniel was appointed a senior advisor resulting in the incident of the lion's den 6:1. His understanding and prayer occurred in that year v1.

When Cyrus returned, possibly 538 BC Daniel as court advisor would have showed him the Isaiah prophecy. Daniel's prayer and witness influenced Cyrus to agree to the return of the captives. Historical records confirm this policy as discovered on the Cyrus Cylinder 536 BC.

The Temple was rebuilt and dedicated in 516 BC, seventy years after destruction, in keeping with the prophecy (586 to 516 BC).

REVELATION 4 - The Coming of Messiah – received 539 BC

9:24 The Work of the Messiah As the prayer for return of the exiles was answered ending the seventy years of exile new revelation was given describing the outworking of events up to the establishment of the Messianic millennium kingdom (compare with 7:13,14). Daniel was told that a further period of seventy 'sevens' would occur for his people and Jerusalem leading to the **coming of the promised Messiah!** We are told to know and understand these things v25.

The Messiah would achieve six requirements to -

• *finish transgression* - remove the failure of the people to keep the Old Covenant - Jesus *was stricken for the transgression of my people Is 53:8;* Jn 1:29

• *put an end to sin* - animal sacrifices could not remove the power of sin - only the sinless sacrifice of Jesus could achieve this Rom 6:6-7; Heb 9:26,28

• *atone for wickedness* - remove the offense of sin before God who presented Jesus *as a sacrifice of atonement for sin through faith in his blood Rom 3:25;* Heb 9:14; 1Pet 1:19 - this could happen in no other way

• *bring in everlasting righteousness* - imputed righteousness of God through faith in Jesus to all who believe Rom 1:17; 3:21,22

• *seal up vision and prophecy* - complete the plan of salvation through the ministry of Jesus Mt 5:17,18; Lk 4:17-21

• *anoint the Most Holy One* - to announce and appoint the Messiah Mt 3:16,17; Jn 1:29-34.

All these Messianic goals were made possible by Jesus during his life, death and resurrection v25-27 – he came to fulfill them Mk 1:14,15. There is no one else who could meet these conditions - *salvation is found in no one else for there is no other name under heaven given to men by which we must be saved Acts 4:12;* Rev 5:2-10.

All six conditions will be completed by the end of the seventieth year in the millennium age when the full number of the Gentiles has come in and the deliverer has come to Zion Rom 11:25-27.

9:24 **Seventy 'sevens' are decreed** – Seven is the number of completeness. Seventy Sabbath cycles is 490 years Lev 25:8.

9:25 **The Decree to Restore** – the period would begin with the decree to restore Jerusalem.

The first decree, as foretold by Isaiah Is 44:24-28 was made in 538 BC when 50,000 Jews returned under Sheshbazzar and Zerubbabel to rebuild the Temple Ezr 1:1-4; 2:1.

Opposition resulted in another decree by Darius 522-486 BC based on the first decree Ezr 4:5; 6:1-6. The Temple was dedicated 516 BC.

Later opposition to the building of the city and walls in the reigns of Xerxes 486-465 BC and Artaxerxes 465-424 BC resulted in the ongoing work being stopped.

A third decree by Artaxerxes in 458 BC due to a change of mind allowed Ezra to return to Jerusalem and re-establish Temple worship and administration Ezr 7:11-28.

A further decree by Artaxerxes in 445 BC allowed Nehemiah to return as governor in 445 BC to complete the building of the city wall and to work with Ezra to re-establish nationhood by 430 BC Neh 2:1-8.

9:25 **Until the Anointed One, the Ruler comes, there will be seven 'sevens' and sixty-two 'sevens'** (that is sixty-nine 'sevens'). This clearly set the time for the Messiah to arrive.

The period would be in three stages –

• **The first seven 'sevens'** – making 49 years, would result in the completion of the rebuilding of Jerusalem and the end of the prophetic word around 400 BC. This was accomplished in times of trouble v25.

• **The second period of sixty-two 'sevens'** – making 434 years would lead to the coming of Messiah.

9:25 **The Anointed One the Ruler comes** - Messiah, the Prince, will come in sixty-nine 'sevens' – making 483 years.

- Daniel saw this as a further period of seventy 'sevens' from the end of the exile and the decree of Cyrus 538 BC for Zerubbabel to rebuild the city and Temple leading to the coming of Messiah and another desolation of the Temple v27. Work on the city was stopped by Artaxerxes Ezr 4:12,21
- Looking back we see that from the instruction of Artaxerxes 458 BC to Ezra to re-establish the Temple worship leads to AD 27 (483 years based on 360 day Hebrew lunar years)
- We can also calculate from the permission of Artaxerxes 445 BC to Nehemiah to rebuild the city wall leads to AD 30 (476 years based on 365.25 day Gregorian solar years).

Each explanation amazingly points to the coming of Jesus the Messiah! He was anointed to ministry AD 27 at his baptism. He entered Jerusalem on Sunday Nisan 9, AD 30 (Palm Sunday) at the Triumphal Entry when the people acclaimed him as king Zec 9:9; Mt 21:1-9; Mk 11:1-11; Lk 19:28-40.

At that time the rulers rejected Jesus and he wept over the city - *they will not leave one stone on another because you did not recognize the time of God's coming to you Lk 19:41-44;* Jn 19:14,15.

Just as people of Jesus' day did not recognize his Messiahship so today many deny the fulfilment of these extraordinary prophetic statements!

9:26 After the sixty two 'sevens', the Anointed One will be cut off and will have nothing! Is 53:8. Five days after this on Friday Nisan 14 AD 30 Jesus was crucified Lk 23:33.

9:26 The people of the ruler who will come will destroy the city and the sanctuary. Forty years later Titus the Roman 'prince' destroyed Jerusalem and the Temple AD 70. He was son of Emperor Vespasian at the time – a prince! This destruction of the Temple was foretold by Jesus forty years before Mt 24:1,2. These two events occurred after the sixty-two 'sevens'.

9:27 He will confirm a covenant with many for one 'seven' Jesus did established the New Covenant during the first half of **one 'seven'** - the term of his earthly ministry. It confirmed the Old Covenant with Abraham and the Jewish people and incorporated people of all nations Rom 15:8. Rejection by Israel came with the denouncing of Stephen and his message by the Sanhedrin (the end of the one 'seven') Acts 7:54. The requirement for future acceptance was given Mt 23:37-39.

9:27 In the middle of the 'seven' he will put an end to sacrifice
The New Covenant of grace established by Jesus was accomplished by the shedding of his blood on the cross putting an end to the need for sacrifice. This was later reinforced by the destruction of the Temple and elimination of the Levitical Sacrificial System in AD 70 v26.
• **The seventieth 'seven'** – while Jesus initiated the messianic goals they have not reached completion. There is a gap before the final week of 'seven' years when the goals will reach fulfilment in the end time at the return of Jesus v24.
The Church Age initiated by Jesus will continue till the 'fullness of the Gentiles has come in' with the rapture of believers in the end time Rom 11:25. The coming Messiah and final redemption of Israel was predicted by the Major Prophets – Isaiah 9:6,7; 11:1; 59:20; Jeremiah 23:5,6; 31:33,34; 33:14-17; Ezekiel 34:23-31 - also foretold by Paul Rom 11:26-29.
9:27 An abomination that causes desolation This personification of evil has occurred in all generations. It reveals the determination of the evil one to raise up a representative of evil to oppose and attempt to usurp the authority of God and attempt to overcome the faithful believers. It is manifest in -
• The desolation of the Temple by the Syrian ruler Antiochus Epiphanes in 167 to 164 BC – as revealed in Daniel's second revelation 8:1-27
• The destruction of the Temple by the Roman general Titus in AD 70 v26; Mt 23:38
• The destruction of Jerusalem and expulsion of Jews by the Roman emperor Hadrian AD 130-135 - he built a pagan city Aelia Capitolina
• It will occur again in the last days as foretold by Jesus - *when you see standing in the holy place the abomination that causes desolation spoken of through the prophet Daniel Mt 24:15.* This prophecy of Jesus referred both to the destruction of Jerusalem and to the end time
• The rebellion and the 'man of lawlessness' was foretold by the apostle Paul - an intense manifestation of evil to be revealed before the return of Jesus and to be overthrown and destroyed by him 2Thes 2:3-12
• John confirmed the antichrist is coming - many have come - *the man who denies that Jesus is the Christ, such a man is the antichrist - he denies the Father and the Son 1Jn 2:18-22*
• John foresaw that in the last days a beast will rise out of the sea that will be the final antichrist Rev 13:1-8. This personification of evil compares with the **little horn** of 8:9-12 and the **eighth king** of Rev 17:11.

• **The End Time – the seventieth 'seven'** requires that the antichrist will appear in a period of Tribulation to persecute God's people. He will attempt to imitate the acts of Jesus. At the midpoint there will be Great Tribulation before he is destroyed at the return of Jesus Christ to complete the six Messianic conditions 9:24,26,27; 11:36-45; Mt 24:13,21,29,30. Jesus will bring in the golden age of the millennium foretold by the prophets Is 2:1-4; 11:1-16; Jer 23:5,6; Ezk 36:22-38; Rev 20:1-6.

This cataclysmic end time event was foretold three times by Daniel 9:27; 11:36; 12:11.

In all situations we are encouraged to be faithful to God who is sovereign over all and is able to rescue from the fiery furnace and deliver from the lions den.

REVELATION 5 - Future Events - received 536 BC

10:1-21 **The pursuit of knowledge** This vision came in conjunction with a time of fasting v2. The messenger wore heavenly attire - but is markedly different to the vision of Jesus v5; Rev 1:13-16. Daniel was again recognized as highly esteemed in the heavenly realms v11; 9:23.

This new revelation was given because *you set your mind to gain understanding and to humble yourself before God v12*. As soon as we pray we will be heard and the answer will surely be given despite delays provided we persist in our pursuit. We may be sure that we will benefit from meditating on the Word of God and seeking to understand his purposes Jos 1:8; Pro 25:2.

The Book of Truth v21 God's purposes were established before the foundations of the earth. His plans are being worked out and cannot be thwarted Is 14:24; 44:24; Mt 25:34; Acts 17:24-28; Eph 4:9-11; Rev 17:8; 20:12.

Heavenly Realms We see in this encounter a glimpse of the battle between good and evil that is being waged in the heavenly realms. The angels of God including the chief princes of heaven Gabriel 9:21 and Michael 10:13 are in conflict with the demonic powers over nations who scheme to frustrate God's purposes v13,20 – they did not want Cyrus to release the Jewish people and did not want Daniel to be informed of the coming of the Messiah. We too are involved - *our struggle is not against flesh and blood but against the rulers, against the authorities, against the powers of this dark world and against the spiritual forces of evil in* *the heavenly realms* - therefore we need to put on the full armor of God in order to stand Eph 6:10-13.

Daniel's three weeks of prayer and fasting was used in the outworking of God's purposes for the redemption of his people 10:12-21.

The Great War This Vision 5 describes the events of Vision 2 with much more detail. The main purpose was to show the people of God that the conflict with the world will be finally overcome with the return of the Messiah.

11:1-4 Persia was ruled by Cyrus II 559-530 BC. The following three kings were likely Cambyses 530-521 BC, Smerdis 521 BC and Darius I 521-485 BC. The fourth was Xerxes 486-464 BC Est 1:1 who made war with and stirred up Greece v2. Alexander the Great of Greece 336-323 BC conquered Persia under Darius III 331 BC. His kingdom was divided after his death among four generals - Ptolemy, Seleucus, Cassander and Lysimachus v4; 8:9.

11:5-20 **Middle East Conflict** The king of the south was Ptolemy I 305-283 BC who took control of Egypt. Seleucus 305-281 BC controlled the north including Syria and extending to Babylon. As described in considerable detail by Gabriel 8:16 and recorded by Daniel conflict, intrigue and war would continue between these two kingdoms for 150 years until Antiochus Epiphanes 175-164 BC seized power in Syria 175 BC. Subsequent history has amazingly confirmed all of the details outlined!

11:21-36 **The Contemptible Person** Antiochus was prevented from conquering Egypt by the presence of the Romans and so turned in vengeance on Jerusalem v29,30. On his return to Syria he became the contemptible person already described 8:23-25 when in 167 to 164 BC he desecrated the Temple and prevented the daily sacrifice v31; 8:13,14. This was only a prelude to the future. The ultimate fulfilment will occur at the end of the age Mt 24:15; Rev 19:19-21.

11:36-45 **Final World Empire** The vision now portrays events at the end time v40. There will be terrible world conflict - a time of great distress leading to the Tribulation.

Antiochus was of the line of Syria and Babylon and is symbolic of the end time antichrist who will rise up as the beast out of the sea representing final world empire and the eighth king Rev 13:1-8; 17:11. He will seek to exalt himself above God v36; he will honor the god of power and wealth v38; he will have the help of the evil one v39 and he will reward those who turn from God v39. He will be resisted by the remaining rulers of the worldly kingdoms and overcome them v40-44. He will rise up against Jerusalem and God's people Israel who will play an important part in this final period v45 when the full number of the Gentiles has come in Rom 11:25-29.

This will involve the Great Tribulation foretold by Jesus and the prophets Mt 24:21; Is 24:1; Jer 30:1-9; Ezk 37:24,25; Zech 14:1-5. As a result many in Israel will repent and be saved 12:1-3.

The present age will end with this confrontation between good and evil and the return of Jesus Christ to begin his millennium rule on earth when *the sovereignty, power and greatness of the kingdoms under the whole heaven will be handed over to the saints 7:14,27;* Is 2:1-5; Hab 2:14.

REVELATION 6 - The Eternal Kingdom – received 536 BC

12:1-10 **The Lamb's Book of Life** v1 At the end of the age *everyone whose name is found in the book* (the Lamb's book of life Rev 20:15) *will be delivered* – they will rise to everlasting life v2. This is the first direct reference to everlasting life and judgment. It is the promise to believing people of all generations and nations. It confirms the salvation of all God's people from both Testaments on the same basis - by grace alone! Rom 4:13.

God's plan of salvation and righteous judgment has been made known to all generations. From the beginning God set before mankind the choice of eternal life or death (separation from God) Gen 2:16,17; 3:22. Enoch warned - *see the Lord is coming with his holy ones to judge everyone and to convict all the ungodly Jude 1:14,15.* He foretold this around 2900 BC. There will be a craving for knowledge and meaning of life searching in ideology, entertainment and religion v5. The answer is only found in Jesus – those who trust in him *will be purified, made spotless and refined v10.* Those who choose to deny God will not understand and will face the final judgment v10.

12:11,12 **The Great Tribulation** will bring in the millennium kingdom. The details of these things are closed and sealed up till the time of the end v4,9.

12:13 **God's Promise of Eternal Life** Daniel was told that he will rise again at the end time! v13. This has always been God's plan for the believer - the 'tree of life' though hid from man through sin was made available through Jesus Christ Gen 3:22; Jn 11:25,26; Rev 2:7. Salvation and eternal life are now open to all those who put their trust in the Messiah.

Conclusion

There is much speculation and opinion about the prophetic Word. The prime purpose of prophecy and interpretation is to promote godly living and motivate believers to tell others about Jesus. A clear understanding of the Book of Daniel confirms that there will be an increase in evil, a final rebellion of mankind against God and the overthrow of worldly political and idological systems. The kingdom of God will be established under the righteous rule of Jesus Christ and possessed by all those who embrace him as Savior and Lord.

While many of the prophecies have meaning for specific generations the current message is for today.

He was given authority, glory and sovereign power; all peoples, nations and men of every language worshiped him. His dominion is an everlasting dominion that will not pass away, and his kingdom is one that will never be destroyed 7:14

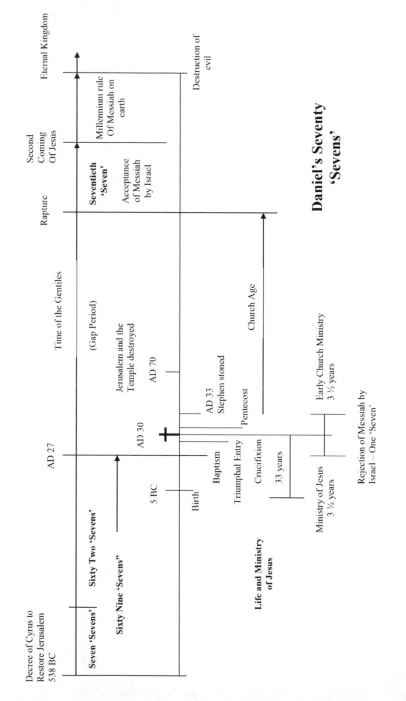

Daniel's Seventy 'Sevens'

Comparing Prophecies of Daniel and Revelation

	Daniel Chapter 2	Daniel Chapter 7	Daniel Chapter 8	Revelation Chapter 17
Kingdom	Statue	Warring Beasts		Kingdom
				1 Egypt v10 3000 BC
				2 Assyria 1100-612 BC
1 Babylon 612 - 539 BC	Gold v37 head	Lion v4		3 Babylon
2 Persia / Media 539 - 332 BC	Silver v39 chest & arms	Bear v5 raised up	Ram v3 2 horns	4 Persia / Media
3 Greece 332 - 63 BC	Bronze v39	Leopard v6 4 heads	Goat v5 4 horns	5 Greece
4 Rome 63 BC-AD 476 AD 330-1453	Iron v40 two legs Iron & clay v41	Terrifying v7 different		6 Rome
				7 A future king
	Feet 10 toes v42	10 horns v7		10 horns v12
		11th horn v8 (little horn)		8 Eighth king v11 Beast 1 - antichrist Beast 2 - false prophet
God of heaven		Ancient of Days v9 Son of Man v13		King of kings v14
God's Kingdom	Rock v44 endure forever	Millennium v14 never be destroyed		Millennium never be destroyed

Hosea

Introduction – Some forty years after the death of Elisha 798 BC God raised up Hosea and Amos as the first of the known writing prophets in Israel to predict the fall of Samaria to Assyria and the dispersion of the people of the northern kingdom among the nations of the world. It meant the end of Israel as a kingdom. The written records of the prophets were preserved by the providence of God to confirm for posterity the rebellion of his people despite his goodness, mercy and patience. They are also relevant to the world today – the same mercy of God is offered and the same denial and rebellion continues.

Author – Hosea, prophet of Israel from around 757–722 BC.

Period – For thirty-five years from the reign of Jeroboam II to the fall of Samaria 722 BC. Hosea was a contemporary of Amos.

Theme – God's great love for his people Israel was unfaithful to God throughout the whole 208 years of the northern monarchy – among 19 kings from Jeroboam to Hoshea not one did what was right in the eyes of the LORD. Hosea pronounced judgment up to the fall of Samaria. Although the message was against Israel (sometimes called Ephraim) the words applied as a warning to Judah as well. There was always a chance to repent.

Condemnation of Israel's Sin

1:1-9 **Example of Unfaithfulness** Hosea was required to marry a woman Gomer, who would be unfaithful to him. She had three children in adultery before he cast her out.

The first son he called Jezreel (God would punish Israel for the slaughter of Ahab's family at Jezreel and their subsequent disobedience 2 K in 10:1-31). The daughter he called Lo-Ruhamah ('unloved' – God would no longer show love to Israel because of their sins). The next son he called Lo-Ammi ('not my people' – Israel would no longer be God's people).

All of this was symbolic of Israel's attitude to God –

- He chose them through Abraham and caused them to multiply
- He delivered them out of bondage in Egypt
- He entered into the Covenant with them to bless them
- He brought them into the Promised Land
- they chose to ignore him; they turned to gods of the world and refused to live by his righteous ways.

The people of Israel were unfaithful to God and deserved the judgment that was about to come on them.

The actions required of Hosea demonstrate the depth of Israel's degradation in following the idols and standards of the local nations and the repugnance of their sin to God. As always the offer of redemption was made.

1:10-11 **Sons of the Living God** God's plan for mankind did not fail with the demise of Israel. His plan extended to include representatives of all people as well as Judah and Israel under one leader. The descendants of Abraham will be as the stars of the heavens and the sand of the seashore v10; Gen 15:5.

The appointment as **sons of the living God** was made possible by the coming of Jesus Christ and the New Covenant v10; Rom 9:25,26; 1Pet 2:10. There is no other name under heaven given to men by which we must be saved Acts 4:12!

2:1 **Family of God** Because of Jesus we are adopted into the family of God v16, 23; Rom 8:12-17; Eph 1:5. We are one with every other believer Eph 2:14-18. O that we might live it!

The comparison of Hosea's children of adultery with Israel is contrasted with the children of God in the new kingdom.

2:2-23 Hosea's rebuke of his outcast wife portrayed God's condemnation and judgment on Israel. The great sin was that the people chose to include man made idols and gods in their worship alongside of the Eternal LORD God v5, 8. So their means of support would be taken away v9. Yet the time would come when God would draw the people back to himself into a new most intimate relationship when they would acknowledge the LORD v14-23.

3:1-5 Hosea was then required to redeem his unfaithful wife and love her again revealing God's continued love and plan for Israel. Hosea's reunion with his wayward wife was compared with the return of God's people into intimate relationship – again foretelling the coming of a king of the line of David –

• the Israelites will return and seek the LORD their God
• they will seek David their king
• they will come trembling to the LORD and to his blessings in the last days v5.

This dramatic series of events foretells the redemption of Israel and their acceptance of Jesus Christ, Messiah in the end time as prophesied Dan 11:45; Ezk 39:28,29; Rom 11:25-29; Rev 14:1.

***4:1-19* God brought a charge against Israel** – they did not acknowledge him and were not faithful to his laws. There was moral, economic and ecological ruin v2,3. The people were destroyed because of lack of knowledge – they excluded God. They ignored the law of God and exchanged their faith for degradation. The extent of their sins is hard to comprehend.

***5:1-15* The Judgment** They had become so corrupt that they could not repent without discipline v3,4. This warning applied to Judah as well as Israel - so God would discipline them v14,15.

***6:1-11* No Repentance** Because of God's compassion, mercy and grace there is always opportunity to return to him with a penitent heart v1-3,6. But Israel were not prepared for true reform, they had broken the Covenant – a reminder of the original sin in human nature 6:7; Gen 2:16,16; 3:22. The harvest for Judah would also come – reaping what they had sowed v11.

***7:1-13* They are always before me** We need to realize that God does see all our deeds - that we are always before him v2 - we will give account. For the unrepentant their rebellion and disobedience are an offense to God - for those who put their trust in him they will be white as snow Is 1:18.

***7:13-16* I longed to redeem them but - they do not cry out from their hearts.** People wail and complain because things don't go their way but ignore the One who supplies all things. They eat and drink but turn away from God v14. Despite God's nature we do not turn to the Most High v16.

***8:1-14* Judgment and Punishment** The command went out – the people have broken God's covenant and rebelled against his law v1. They sow the wind and reap the whirlwind - their deeds are empty and they court disaster v7.

9:1-17 When we continue to ignore God and his ways life becomes increasingly meaningless and we suffer the consequences. Israel was rejected - conquered by Assyria in 722 BC and became wanderers among the nations v17; Deu 28:25.

***10:1-15* The Source of Righteousness** Israel was past reform and had to receive the yoke of discipline. Judah could be spared if they took notice of what would happen to their northern neighbor and repented. We can receive God's righteousness and the fruit of his unfailing love if we seek him. We must be prepared to change our attitude to God and his Word – ***sow to yourselves righteousness* -** break up your unplowed ground v12.

Then as we continue to seek him he will shower his blessings, including his righteousness on us. These judgments against the people of the Old Covenant are relevant as warnings to the nations today, who ignore God and compromise his ways – we live before the same God and will answer to him whether we acknowledge him or not 1Cor 10:11,12.

God's Love and Compassion

11:1-12 God's plan for Israel began with Abraham and progressed through Moses when he delivered them out of slavery to be his people, demonstrating his great love for them. But the more he called them the further they went from him v1,2. Despite their rejection, his love and compassion were for them. God would have to discipline them out of love; then he could bring them back to their homeland. The conflict between God's justice and mercy was ultimately resolved by the atoning sacrifice of Jesus on the cross Heb 10:11,12.

12:1-14 **Conditions for Repentance** Jacob the patriarch was an example of the way to pursue God. From the beginning he sought God's blessing – he struggled, overcame, wept and begged until he found God; he talked with him and received his blessing v3-5. God's people can find God *but they must return to him, maintain love and justice and wait for God always v6.* The people were not prepared to do this v14.

13:1-16 **Repentance requires firstly acknowledging God alone –** *I am the LORD your God - you shall acknowledge no God but me, no Savior except me v4.* In the midst of the judgment comes mercy – repentance leads not only to forgiveness but to eternal life – possible through faith in Jesus v14; 1Cor 15:55-57.

14:1-9 During the discipline the people needed to recognize that their sins were the cause of their downfall and offer 'words of repentance' - forgive all our sins v1,2. If so they would be restored – healed, loved, blossoming and fruitful once more.

The Ways of the LORD

14:9 These words are a summary of the message of Hosea and of the Bible as a whole. They are also a guide for our lives -

The ways of the LORD are right;
the righteous walk in them v9.

Joel – YHWH is God

Introduction – God uses natural events to draw our attention to himself. This is evident throughout the world today. As people of Joel's day did not respond to the warning so we must face the consequences of ignoring God's warnings in our experience. The message was addressed to Judah, Jerusalem, Zion 2:1; 3:1,17 with no mention of the northern kingdom of Israel. The events at the time of Joel's prophecy heralded the pending destruction of Jerusalem and the end of Israel as a kingdom, both north and south.

Author – Joel, the unknown prophet of Judah.

Period – Spoken to the people of Judah possibly around 600 BC.

Theme – **The Valley of Decision** Future events were foreseen - the day of the Lord when all people will face judgment in the Valley of Decision 1:15; 3:12-14.

The Day of the LORD is to be compared with the Second Coming of Jesus to judge mankind. God's judgment on sin is certain Dan 7:9,10; Mt 25:31-46; Rev 20:11-15.

Because of God's loving nature there will always be an invitation to repent for all those who turn to him.

The Coming of the Holy Spirit Joel foretold the coming of the Holy Spirit in fullness with the announcement of salvation for all those from every nation who will call upon the Lord Jesus Christ Acts 2:1-4,28-32. His words are relevant today.

Pending Judgment

1:1-12 **A Plague of Locusts** swept through Judah and left the land devastated. God called Joel to tell the people that this was a sign of pending judgment. God speaks through world events, climatic disasters and national conflicts in our time. A powerful army would come and devastate the land like the locusts had already done v6.

1:13-20 **Repentance** was required if this military catastrophe was to be averted. The leaders must make genuine commitment to return to God and his ways. The day of the LORD was near v15; 2:28-32.

2:1-11 **The Day of the LORD** This judgment was pending. The army would be unstoppable and would strike fear into the hearts of the people Rev 6:15-17.

The LORD will lead them Although the army would be a foreign force they were God's instrument of discipline on his people 2:11. Nebuchadnezzar led the first of three assaults on Jerusalem in 605 BC with final destruction of Jerusalem and the Temple in 586 BC.

2:12-17 Return to Me Even now the invitation to return to the LORD was given. But it would have to be with a sincere heart and not just outward show. People must turn to God – pray, repent with fasting, weeping and mourning - elders, children, mothers, bridegrooms, priests. This offer was based on the nature of God who is *gracious and compassionate, slow to anger and abounding in love* always ready to forgive v13; Ex 33:19; 34:6,7. God does not change, but he does relent from sending the calamity – he withdraws the punishment that is due!

2:18-27 The LORD's Response In answer to the genuine repentance of the people God would drive away the army and send abundant showers of spiritual and physical blessing. *I will repay you for the years the locusts had eaten v25.* Repentance did not happen and so the people went into exile.

God will always restore the sinner who genuinely repents and turns to him - he will build a new life of blessing which will cause them to praise the name of the LORD. This applies to the individual as well as the nation. It has been the experience of many who have called to God in desperate situations and have been forgiven and restored to a new life.

The Day of the LORD

2:28-31 The New Kingdom A time will come when God will 'pour out' his Spirit on all people. This indicates the intimacy with which God seeks to relate with those who honor him and was made possible by the death of Jesus to atone for sin.

Pentecost When Jesus returned to the Father after the ascension the Father sent the Holy Spirit as promised, in response to the high priestly prayer of Jesus *that all of them may be one, Father just as you are in me and I am in you - may they also be in us so that the world may believe that you have sent me Jn 17:20-23.* Fulfilment of God's promise began at Pentecost when the Holy Spirit came on the disciples and all of the believers in the upper room Acts 2:1-21. This was *a seal, the promised Holy Spirit, who is a deposit guaranteeing our inheritance until the redemption of those who are God's possession – to the praise of his glory Eph 1:13,14.*

This new life and the gift of the Holy Spirit are available to all who will *repent and be baptized - in the name of Jesus Christ for the forgiveness of your sins and you will receive the gift of the Holy Spirit Acts 2:38,39.* Complete fulfilment will come with the return of Jesus.

2:32 The offer of salvation is made available to all mankind - *everyone who calls on the name of the LORD will be saved v32.* This is preparing the way for the Great and Dreadful Day of the LORD when heavenly signs will herald the return of the Lord Jesus Christ to judge the world Mt 24:29-31; Rev 19:13-16.

3:1-16 All nations will be judged While Joel spoke directly to the people of Judah and the judgment of the time like many prophecies the LORD gave warning to future generations.

There will be universal conflict before all mankind appears in the Valley of Decision before the Judge to determine what each person has done with their lives and to receive the eternal consequences of their decisions Rev 20:7-15.

The history of the rise and fall of nations demonstrates the certainty of the eventual justice and judgment of God. The continual corruption, greed, self-centeredness and merciless domination by leaders of nations confirms the sinful nature of the human heart Jer 17:9.

The Valley of Jehoshaphat 'the LORD judges' v2 equates with Armageddon 'Mount of Megiddo' overlooking the Plain of Ezdraeldon southeast of Mt Carmel where the final battle of the nations will be gathered against Israel - to be defeated by the King of kings Zech 12:11; Rev 16:16; 19:11-16,19.

3:17-21 The LORD dwells in Zion God is sovereign over the universe and his purposes are being worked out. After the end time he will dwell with his people chosen from all nations of the world and their fortunes will be restored.

The mountains will drip with new wine and the hills will flow with milk v18 This indicates the prosperity and blessing of the new kingdom. *A fountain will flow out of the LORD'S house v18* because the LORD will supply all their need! Rev 21:3-5.

Amos – 'burden bearer'

Introduction – Amos lived in Tekoa, 15 km south of Jerusalem and was called from his secular life as a shepherd to go to Israel in the north and proclaim God's judgment some forty years before it happened in 722 BC.
Author – Amos, shepherd of Judah who prophesied against Israel 7:14,15.
Period – Around 760 BC during the evil reign of Jeroboam II. Amos was a contemporary of Hosea.
Theme – The people failed to honor God and keep his Laws They lived in luxury, self-indulgence and pride with injustice, as the rich and powerful oppressed the poor, weak and helpless. God expressed hate for the formality of religion and abhorred their arrogance, independence and self-reliance.
Righteous judgment was unavoidable as his call to repentance was refused. God's plan for mankind will be fulfilled with a faithful remnant from all nations. The surrounding nations will also be judged. The same requirement for justice and ultimate accountability will be applied to all nations and people.

Judgment against Israel's neighbors
1:1 to 2:3 **The LORD spoke from Zion**, Jerusalem, the city of the Temple. Judgment would come on the nations that showed no mercy for Israel when Assyria would destroy Samaria in 722 BC. They would gloat and take advantage even though their own sins were as great.
This included Damascus, capital of Aram (Syria); Gaza, capital of Philistia; Tyre, capital of Phoenicia; Edom on the southern boarder of Judah (descended from Esau); Ammon on the east and Moab on the south-east (both descended from Lot).
For three sins - even for four refers to the 'many sins' of the people 1:9.
Judgment on Israel and Judah
2:4,5 **Judah** Judgment would come on Judah *because they have rejected the law of the LORD and have not kept his decrees.* Instead of leading the nations to God they had adopted the idols and ways of the nations.
2:6-16 **Israel** Judgment would come on Israel because in addition to the sins of Judah they followed and exceeded the evil ways of the surrounding nations. The wealthy were oppressing the poor and denying justice. History of the deliverance from Egypt under Moses where God

had provided for them and the warnings of the prophets to turn from their ways were recounted but the people did not respond, so judgment was imminent.

3:1-5 The case against Judah and Israel was made. They were *chosen of all the families of the earth v2*. Yet though they had received the Covenant with all the blessings they had not kept the Covenant conditions.

3:6,7 When disaster comes to a city has not the LORD caused it? God is sovereign over the universe. Nothing happens outside of his determined will and knowledge Mt 10:29. His hand is in every activity to speak to the people of the earth Is 45:7.

Here is the interface between God's sovereignty and the responsibility of man Rom 9:16-18. We cannot fully understand his thoughts and ways Is 55:8,9 but we can rest in the confidence that *in all things God works for the good of those who love him Rom 8:28*. We must know that he is with us in everything, for good and bad Is 45:7. He always leads his people in the ways of truth Rom 9:23,24. There is purpose behind every activity and event – we can learn from every situation and we must take note of the warnings Is 14:24,26,27; Jer 29:11-13.

3:8-15 A piece of an ear Because of their unfaithfulness destruction would be so severe that hardly a remnant would be left v12.

4:1-13 **Prepare to meet your God** The superficial religion was unacceptable to God. He had warned them through world events – lack of food, withheld rain, blight on the crops – he even sent plagues as in Egypt and loss of life – but still they did not take notice or repent (God caused an earthquake two years after this prophecy 1:1). So judgment was inevitable v12.

The Creator and Sustainer of the universe who maintains climate and controls the spheres - who treads the high places and also reveals his thoughts to man so that we are without excuse - the LORD God Almighty was announcing his intentions v12,13.

Prepare to meet your God v12 This instruction is critical for all people to consider because the just nature of God requires that each person will encounter the Creator and will be called to give account for their worldview and their actions Mt 12:36; Lk 16:2. As this was a fearful event for both Israel and Judah as their cities were destroyed and the people taken off into a lifetime of captivity so it will be for those who live their lives in denial of God 3:12; Mt 25:31-46.

5:1-17 **Final call to repentance** God's mercy and compassion are revealed. In the declaration of pending judgment the call to repentance was repeated - *Seek me and live! v4,6*; 2Pet 3:9. They were reminded of the fearsome nature of the One making the appeal v8 -
• Pleiades is now known to be an open star cluster (how to bind it?) and Orion is tightly bound (how to loose it?)! Job 38:31,32
• darkness is the absence of energy (light) Ps 139:11,12
• who created and maintains the evaporative water cycle that sustains life on earth Ecc 1:7.
These are incredible scientific statements coming through the lips of a village shepherd 2,600 years ago!
A summary of their offenses was made - still they ignored the call v11-17.

5:18-27 **The Day of the LORD** The luxury, self-indulgence and injustice of the people was great. They looked to the day of the LORD as furthering their own benefits. God expressed his hate for the formality, irreverence and noise of meaningless songs when the injustice and unrighteousness of their actions denied their words v24.

6:1-14 **Loss of High Calling** There was no sense of the loss of their high calling as the people of God v6. The 'ruin of Joseph' - Israel was often called by the name of the largest tribe Ephraim after the youngest son of Joseph Gen 48:14 - an appeal was made to the example of the selfless life of Joseph.
When people ignore the wonder of the Creation and assume mindless evolution from innate preexisting matter with no purpose or destiny they turn their backs on their high calling as beings created in the image of God with eternal destiny.
God abhorred Israel's pride, arrogance, independence and self-reliance. So he would stir up a nation against them v8. This applied to both kingdoms - Zion (Jerusalem) and Samaria v1.

7:1-17 **Five Pictures of Israel's Future Judgment** A plague of locusts v1, a fire v4 and a plumb line v7.
Amos was told by the priest to stop his harsh prophecies but the message intensified v17.

8:1-10 A basket of ripe fruit - ready for judgment.

8:11,12 **A Famine of Hearing the Words of the LORD** People who reject God look for direction and meaning in life which can only be found in the Word of God. They search for spiritual reality but cannot find it. The religions and philosophies of the mind of man do not provide lasting fulfilment and wellbeing. Even those who have come to believe, suffer when they neglect the regular reading of God's Word Ps 119:16.

9:1-4 Destruction of the Temple Amos prayed that the first two events might not happen and the LORD relented showing the power of prayer. Because the people had departed from God's law (the plumb line) and refused to respond to his call to repentance (the ripe fruit) then judgment (the fall of the Temple) would come upon them v1. Hearts hardened to God are antagonistic to his Word. They only hear what pleases them and promotes their own cause 7:10-16.

9:5,6 The Lord, the LORD Almighty The nature and character of the One making this declaration is again revealed - his power, majestic presence, creative life-sustaining force - his infinite knowledge 5:8.

9:7-10 The Sovereign LORD who has dominion over all nations will minister judgment on Israel.

9:11-12 David's 'fallen tent' v11 referred to the tabernacle set up by David to house the Ark of the Covenant 2Sam 6:17. Speaking through the prophet God indicated that he sought a relationship with individuals as he had established with David rather than a Temple and outward show. This relationship is the expectation of Jew and Gentile – from all nations of the world and all generations, who believe in the living God.

9:13-15 The Days are Coming While the LORD Almighty pronounced judgment on sin, his ultimate plan for a faithful people who will honor him and live by his ways will be fulfilled. *I will return and restore David's fallen tent, its ruins I will rebuild – that the remnant of men may seek the LORD and all the Gentiles who bear my name says the LORD who does these things that have been known for ages Acts 15:16,17.* ***The reaper will be overtaken by the plowman and the planter by the one treading grapes*** *v13* This indicates the abundance of the blessing of those who are included in the coming eternal kingdom of God v13; Eph 2:6,7.

Obadiah – 'servant of YHWH'

Introduction – Edom were descendants of Esau, son of Isaac, brother of Jacob. He despised his birthright and sold it for a pot of stew Gen 25:19-34. There was continued conflict between Edom and Israel (descendants of Jacob) Gen 27:41. They refused Israel access to their territory on the way to the Promised Land. Edom was located on the southern border of Judah Num 20:21.

Author – Obadiah, prophet of Judah after 586 BC.

Period – The plundering of Jerusalem was past v11. The conquest by Babylon begun in 605 BC, continued in 597 BC with complete destruction in 586 BC. Obadiah prophesied against Edom as one of the 'poor' left behind in the city.

Theme – Judgment on Edom They were proud, irreverent and self-reliant like their forefather Esau Gen 25:32; 28:8; 36:2 and participated in the plundering of Jerusalem. So they came under the judgment of God. There is a day of accountability for all people! Rev 20:112-15.
The future kingdom of the LORD was foretold Rev 11:15.

1:1-14 **Judgment for pride and violence** God is sovereign over all nations on earth. He will require all people to account for their thoughts, words and actions Mt 12:36,37. Judgment on Edom would be severe v6. They stood by when Jerusalem was attacked by Babylon and despised their fellow man. They took part in plundering and persecution. We need compassion for all persecuted people and not take advantage of their misfortunes.

1:15,16 **Day of the LORD** As the day of reckoning came for Edom so all nations and people will appear before God – *as you have done it will be done to you; your deeds will return upon your own head.* God's universal law of justice and righteousness is written in our hearts. We all have a sense of right and wrong, good and bad and a desire for justice, especially for ourselves. According to that law, written in the heart, each person will be required to give account Rom 1:18-23; 2:14,15; 2Cor 5:10. Be forever thankful for the Gospel and the righteousness of God that is revealed by faith in Christ from first to last! Rom 1:16,17.

1:17-21 **Kingdom of the LORD** The fulfilment of all our aspirations and God's promises will occur when *the kingdom of the world becomes the kingdom of our Lord and of his Christ and he will reign forever Rev 11:15.*

Jonah

Introduction – It is possible that Jonah was called to Nineveh to purge Assyria before God used them to conquer Israel. Many who heard Jonah's message would have been alive when Samaria fell in 722 BC. At the time Assyria were at the height of power and unlikely to respond to Jonah without the power and influence of God.

Author – Jonah, prophet of Israel around 760 BC 2Kin 14:25.

Period – Jonah was a prophet during the evil reign of Jeroboam II. Samaria was conquered 30 years after Jeroboam's death.

Theme – The Reluctant Prophet Many lessons from the life of Jonah apply today. All things work towards the completion of God's plan for mankind including the salvation of people. He intervenes in the affairs of the world – he called Jonah, pursued him, rescued him and caused him to complete his mission. It was God who sent and equipped Jonah and turned the hearts of the king and people of Nineveh. God is patient giving every opportunity to respond – in this case his patience was with Jonah! After spending three days in the specially prepared fish Jonah preached salvation to the foreign city of Nineveh and there was a great response.

Salvation for all who respond This event in the life of Jonah reveals the universal nature of God's plan for the ultimate salvation of people of all nations who will acknowledge him. This is motivation to tell others about salvation through Jesus.

A profile of the person God uses -

1:1-2 **A Comfortable Prophet** Jonah was safe, happy, comfortable – a faithful believer. God disturbed his comfort by giving him a task.

Many would want to live comfortable self-centered lives. We are not here to be comfortable.

• God wants to develop our character and this requires effort
• He wants to build our faith and this requires testing
• He wants us to be involved with him in extending the kingdom and this requires commitment
• God challenges our comfort and inaction - we are destined to do great things and become special people.

If you are on earth it is for a purpose.

What is the reason God continues to give you life?

1:3 **A Reluctant Prophet** When God said 'Go' Jonah went in the opposite direction. He was not afraid of the task but did not want to see the people of Nineveh spared 4:2 – they were the enemy Mt 5:43-45. We may find many reasons to avoid doing what we are called to do. God challenges our fears, our likes and dislikes and our prejudices. We must confront our lethargy and reluctance. Greatness comes through decisions and plans, actions and effort. Great things happen when you step out in faith.

Bad things happen because good people do nothing. Good things happen when people answer the call - respond to the occasion - make the effort. The Good Samaritan came, saw, took pity, took action and provided what it cost - the leaders passed by Lk 10:33-35.

1:4-16 **A Troublesome Prophet** Jonah went his own way – he boarded a boat and went to sleep. His disobedience caused trouble for himself and others – he was a poor witness.

1:17 **A Symbolic Prophet** The LORD provided a great fish – Jonah was inside the fish for three days and nights. This experience was symbolic of the time Jesus spent in the tomb and was given to the people as a sign to confirm that he is the Messiah Mt 12:40; Lk 11:30. We also see God's sovereignty over all creation and creatures.

2:1-10 **A Repentant Prophet** When we are in distress the LORD hears our cry. Like many people Jonah had to get into great difficulty before he turned to God.

Although Jonah resisted his call God was patient in bringing him to the place where he would again submit to faithful service. Jonah recalled that those who hold on to worthless things of the world *forfeit the grace that could be theirs v8* – they miss out on their potential. We must look for our strengths, weakness, opportunities and threats - turn our weaknesses into strengths and our threats into opportunities.

3:1-10 **An Able Prophet** Once Jonah was willing to submit, the call came a second time. He obeyed and capably preached the message of pending destruction. The people of Nineveh including the king responded by calling on God and turning from their evil ways. While we are required to make our best efforts in the work of the kingdom we must always remember that it is God who gives the ability and the increase.

Great things are possible when we bring what we have, our abilities, resources and willingness and submit them into the hands of the sovereign LORD Mt 14:15-21.

Salvation open to all Jesus also used this example of the repentance of Nineveh to demonstrate that salvation is available to all who will accept it Mt 12:41. Only those who reject it will be condemned Jn 3:17-21.

4:1 **A Disgruntled Prophet** Jonah was displeased that the people of this foreign city were given the opportunity to repent. He knew that salvation was the likely result because of God's gracious and compassionate nature. When we are dissatisfied with things we become angry. Although Jonah knew God's nature he had not come to the place where he could embrace God's sovereign grace and will. It is only when we become involved with God that we grow in our understanding of his nature, character and ways Jer 33:2,3.

4:2-9 **A Merciful God** The God who judges and punishes is also the God who loves according to his infinite wisdom and knowledge. We have no basis for being dissatisfied with God's will especially when it relates to blessing other people.

Have you any right to be angry? v4. God challenged Job's attitude. God treated Jonah with patience and grace. He provided shade which made Jonah happy then took it away which made him angry again. Jonah's sorrow for the vine related to his own selfish comfort yet he had no concern for the unsaved people or their livestock.

The right attitude We also understand the need to have a positive, accepting attitude to other people. We may not agree with them or follow their lifestyles but we accept them and show the love and example of Jesus towards them Jn 4:7; 19:1-10.

4:10,11 Should I not be concerned about that great city? v11. God is concerned with the lives of every person, independent of their beliefs and persuasions. He is not willing that any should perish but that all should repent and come to eternal life Ezk 18:23,32; 2Pet 3:9. When we begin to feel and see others with the heart of God we are motivated to prayer, to witness and to mission.

Micah

Introduction – Micah warned Israel and Judah of pending destruction in the twenty years leading to the fall of Samaria to Assyria in 722 BC. He was a contemporary of Isaiah in Judah and Hosea in Israel.

Author – Micah, prophet of Judah from 740–700 BC.

Period – Micah prophesied in Judah during the reigns of Jotham, Ahaz and Hezekiak over forty years.

Theme – Justice demands judgment - that God's chosen people, Judah and Israel be conquered and go into exile because of their failures. They turned from God to idols and followed immoral and self-centered ways. They failed *to act justly and to love mercy and to walk humbly with God 6:8*.

The Messianic King Micah foresaw the coming of Jesus the Messiah, the forgiveness of sin, the millennium kingdom on earth foretold by the prophets and the eternal kingdom of God 7:8-20.

Judgment against Israel and Judah

1:1-16 The prophecies were against both Israel (Samaria) and Judah (Jerusalem). They were pronounced by the Sovereign LORD to all the people of the earth. God's justice and mercy are universal. It is the LORD who brought the judgment v3.

The capital of Israel was relocated from Shechem to Samaria in 885 BC 45 years after the death of Solomon and the dividing of the United Kingdom.

Judah retained the capital of Jerusalem and the Temple.

Israel immediately adopted heathen idols which led the people away from God 1Kin 12:25-30. They were first to suffer destruction because of their complete rejection of God. Samaria became a heap of rubble v6. This occurred in 722 BC.

However Jerusalem came under judgment too because they became as corrupt as Samaria v9,12,13.

Plans for Disaster and for Deliverance

2:1-13 Mankind makes selfish plans for their own benefit. Often they adopt evil ways. God sees the evil intentions and makes plans to discipline v3. Worldly advisers refute the Word of God and speak words that people want to hear. Evildoers will be punished. Those who seek

God and his ways will be gathered together as God's people under one king v13.

***3:1-12* Leaders and Teachers** Those responsible for leading and teaching come under greater condemnation because of their knowledge and influence. But people are still responsible for their deeds if they follow evil ways.

Micah acknowledged the source of his power to serve was the Spirit of the LORD v8.

Jerusalem also became a heap of rubble in 586 BC v12.

The Mountain of the LORD

***4:1-13* The Last Days** Mountains represent security and the presence of God. Jerusalem was called Mt Zion, the Citadel (stronghold). It became known as the Mountain of God, the earthly dwelling place of God - where the Tabernacle was kept during the reign of king David 2Sam 6:17; Ps 2:6; 48:2; 76:2 – where the Temple was built by Solomon 1Kin 6:1.

Micah foresaw the day when God would again establish his people in Jerusalem. In the last days - he will call together people from all nations to worship and walk in the ways of the LORD v2. The LORD will teach people from all nations his ways and they will walk in his paths Ps 2:4-9; Rev 2:27.

It will be a time of justice, righteousness and peace v3,4 – the millennium reign of Christ on earth, foretold also by the prophets v8; Isaiah 2:1-5; 9:6,7; 11:1; Jeremiah 23:5,6; 33:11-17; Ezekiel 34:23-31 and Daniel 12:11,12. All of these promises to God's people have yet to be fulfilled Rev 20:1-4.

The Eternal Kingdom v5-8 This millennium kingdom on earth will lead to the eternal kingdom where the LORD will reign forever Rev 21:1-3.

5:1-5 The Ruler of the Eternal Kingdom

• He will come from Bethlehem of the line of Judah v2

• His origins are from ancient (eternal) times - he will be of God v2

• He will be the Good Shepherd in the majesty of the LORD and will reign to the ends of the earth v4

• He will be their peace - the means by which they will know peace v5 – peace with God and mankind Eph 2:14.

This prophecy spoke of Jesus and will be fulfilled when Jesus returns as the King of kings and Lord of lords Rev 19:16.

5:5-15 The Nations of the World In that day v10, before the millennium rule, the nations will rise up against God's people. They are represented by Assyria and Nimrod of old v5,6 Gen 10:8-12. The LORD will deliver his people – all their foes will be destroyed v9. All those who have rejected God and ignored his ways will know the wrath of God.

The Case against Mankind

6:1-5 The Moral Attributes of God revealed in the Bible include righteousness, justice, truth, goodness, fairness and equality. He continually seeks the welfare of mankind Ps 11:7; 145:17. His holiness means separation from all that is evil. His justice requires judgment on sin.

He is *compassionate, gracious, slow to anger, abounding in love and faithfulness, maintaining love to thousands and forgiving wickedness, rebellion and sin - yet will not leave the guilty unpunished Ex 34:6,7.*

It is only as we understand these moral attributes that we come to recognize the offense of sin against God and the magnitude of his grace through the death of our Lord Jesus Christ.

God called Israel before the court to answer his charge against them v1. He reviewed his goodness, provision and presence in their time of testing v4,5.

Walking with God

6:6-8 Righteousness before God Human nature pursues formal ritual, physical engagement and outward show. The requirements for a life lived in the Presence of God are -

He has shown you, O man, what is good
And what does the LORD require of you?
To act justly and to love mercy
And to walk humbly with your God Is 57:15.

6:9-16 The LORD is calling Yet the people did not acknowledge him or follow his ways - there was a case to answer. Because of their sin they would suffer ruin v16.

We will each give account for our lives before the righteous judge - *for we must all appear before the judgment seat of Christ, that each one may receive what is due him for the things done while in the body, whether good or bad 2Cor 5:10.* We must understand as David did that we will not be able to contend with God but can only fall on his infinite mercy and grace, now revealed through the Lord Jesus Christ Ps 51:4.

7:1-6 **The time of confusion** The consequences of rejecting God and following self-centered and evil ways are corruption, impoverishment, misery, family breakdown and separation of brethren Mt 10:35 – the opposite of what God intends Mt 6:33.

God's Eternal Plan
7:7-9 **God My Savior** Despite the threat of impending judgment Micah was able to rejoice in the hope he had in God. Those who put trust in God know that while they have sinned they will not fall – they will rise! Instead of being the judge and prosecutor in court God will be their advocate and plead their cause! 1Jn 2:1,2. We will receive his righteousness – right standing in his Presence through faith in Christ alone Rom 1:16,17; 3:21,22. The enemy has no influence over us when we are secure in this truth Rom 8:31-39.

7:10-19 **Sins will be Pardoned** The day for rebuilding will come for those who seek the LORD. People from all nations will come before God. Sin will be pardoned and transgression forgiven – God will *hurl all our iniquities into the depths of the sea v19*. This great promise was only made possible by the atoning death of Jesus Heb 10:14. The mercy of God has obliterated the certificate of debt that was against us. The powers and authorities that were against us were disarmed, defeated, their hold over us was broken – this was the triumph of the cross that set us free from the penalty and power of sin Acts 3:19; Col 2:13-15.

7:20 **God's Pledge to Abraham** God chose Abraham calling him to leave his home in Ur and move to Canaan. He was faithful in responding and so became the **'father of the faithful'** Gen 17:5. The call involved seven promises including that all peoples on earth would be blessed through him Gen 12:1-3. This promise was fulfilled for all peoples on earth by the death of Jesus on the cross. *Christ redeemed us from the curse of the law by becoming a curse for us - in order that the blessing given to Abraham might come to the Gentiles through Christ Jesus, so that by faith we might receive the promise of the Spirit Gal 3:13,14.*
Micah was confident God would be true to his pledge to Abraham! We may be confident of salvation and eternal life by faith in Jesus 1Jn 5;11,12.

Nahum – 'relief'

Introduction – Nineveh, capital of Assyria responded to the message of Jonah around 760 BC and was used to conquer Samaria (Israel) in 722 BC. Over the next 110 years Assyria was dominant and brought the nations of the Fertile Crescent including Judah under tribute. Sennacherib sought to conquer Jerusalem in 717 BC but was prevented as a result of Hezekiah's prayer for deliverance 2Kin 19:20. Assyria dominated from 1000 BC until overthrown by Babylon in 612 BC.

Author – Nahum, prophet of Judah and contemporary of Jeremiah.

Period – Prophecy against Nineveh in the years before its fall.

Theme – God's punishment on Assyria for flouting God's mercy and ruthlessly treating the surrounding nations. Whereas they responded to Jonah they refused to listen to Nahum and were conquered.

Responsibility of Leaders – Those who have positions of authority and leadership will be held accountable.

Righteousness of God

1:1-7 **The Moral Attributes of God** are revealed in his righteous acts Ex 3:14; Mt 5:48; 1Jn 4:8 -

Jealous means God is vigilant in maintaining his holiness and requiring his created beings to honor his character. He also has great love for his chosen people Ex 19:3-6; 1Pet 2:9.10.

Vengeance means the just response to denial of his Presence and disregard for his laws. He will avenge refusal to follow his ways.

Wrath is the ultimate response to constant rejection and abuse of his boundless grace v2.

Vengeance must take into account all issues and can only rest with our all-knowing God Heb 10:30.

The LORD is slow to anger and great in power v3

• God's mercy is revealed in his patience with the individual, giving every opportunity to respond to him 2Pet 3:8-10

• God's power is seen in his sovereign authority over all creation – nature and people. Nothing can frustrate his will and purpose - *My purpose will stand and I will do all that I please Is 46:10.*

The LORD will not leave the guilty unpunished v3 Justice is inevitable. Knowledge of this truth is written in the human heart in our desire for justice, especially for ourselves.

God is not vindictive – he takes no pleasure in suffering but rather that we may turn from wickedness and enjoy his favor Ezk 18:23,32; 33:11. He also declares the blessing of obedience and the consequence of rejection of his ways Deut 28:1-14,15-68.

1:7 The LORD is good, a refuge in times of trouble. He cares for those who trust in him This quality of the goodness of God draws the individual to him in trust and dependence and is supremely revealed in the cross of Jesus Rom 5:8.

1:8-14 **An End of Nineveh** Destruction was about to fall on Assyria and their idols. This would give relief to God's people in Judah who were under the yoke but it would be short-lived because they did not respond to the opportunity. Jerusalem fell 25 years after the fall of Nineveh.

In all of the prophecies God's justice and mercy are revealed – the certainty of accountability and the offer of redemption v12.

1:15 **Good News** The aspiration of the human being is to know peace. This was announced with the birth of Jesus and will be fulfilled at his second coming Is 52:7; Lk 2:14; Rev 21:3,4.

2:1-13 **Nature of the Fall** Destruction would be total and complete and the city exiled v11. The destroyer would be sent by the LORD in the form of the combined forces of Babylon in the south and Media in the north v13.

3:1-19 **Reasons for the Fall** Assyria was particularly vicious and vindictive. While they administered justice and discipline on Israel they were arrogant and without mercy, lusting for slaughter and plunder. They enslaved nations destroying national identity by relocating people from their homelands.

Responsibility of Leaders We must understand that all authority is in the hand of the sovereign God – *You set up kings and you depose them Dan 2:21;* Pro 8:15; Is 40:23. When given opportunity to lead we must act responsibly and with justice and concern for the individual knowing that we will be held accountable for the privilege given to us by the LORD. Assyria would suffer the fate they had inflicted on Egypt (who were invaded by Esarhaddon in 675 BC) v8 - they would be fatally wounded because of their endless cruelty and witchcraft v4,19. This applies to all in authority.

Habakkuk

Introduction – Nineveh, capital of Assyria fell to Babylon in 612 BC. After the death of the good king Josiah, Judah was ruled successively by four evil kings Jehoahaz, Jehoiakim, Jehoiachin and Zedekiah leading up to the fall of Jerusalem in 586 BC which Habakkuk foresaw. During this twenty-six year period Habakkuk spoke against the evils of Judah. He was a contemporary of Jeremiah.

Author – Habakkuk, prophet of Judah.

Period – Around 600 BC before the fall of Jerusalem.

Theme – This revelation came in response to two questions that concern us all. God's righteous purposes are being worked out through history. Evil will not go unpunished.

The righteous will live by their faith in God Heb 11:6. The message of Habakkuk is of direct relevance to all ages and is applicable today.

1:1-4 **Why is there injustice in the world?** Habakkuk wanted to know why unjust people seem to prosper over the righteous. This question may have been prompted by the unseemly death of Josiah 2Chro 35:20-27. It is good to know we may ask questions of God. There are many things we cannot understand, yet the sincere prayer of the persistent inquirer will always be answered.

1:5-11 **Judgment on sin is inevitable** God revealed that he was preparing the nation of Babylon to bring judgment on his people of Judah - within 20 years! Circumstances outside our influence are often used by God to gain our attention or to bring discipline in our lives. We may not understand at the time but the result will always lead to maturity Jas 1:2-4.

1:12,13 **Why does evil seem to prosper?** Habakkuk acknowledged the sovereignty of God – he is from everlasting – he is holy - he is merciful, punishes wrongdoing, executes judgment and cannot permit evil without punishment. Already Habakkuk was finding answers to his question as he pondered what he knew and meditated before the LORD. He was surprised because he thought Babylon was more evil than Judah. Like many he considered that sin is a matter of degrees. We also compare our goodness with the standard of others rather than with the character and nature of the Almighty whose *eyes are too pure to look on evil; you cannot tolerate wrong v13*; Mt 5:48.

1:13-17 **Why do you tolerate evil?** Why does it take so long before justice seems to be done?

2:1 **Waiting on God** Having asked his questions Habakkuk stayed at his watch (got on with the job) and settled in to a time of waiting on God. One of our great problems is impatience. We want things to happen now – we don't like to wait. This reveals the shallowness of our prayer and devotional life. Because of this we miss out on many blessings. We are often asked to enter into God's presence to wait on him. We ignore this invitation at our loss. *Be still and know that I am God; I will be exalted among the nations Ps 46:10;* 37:7; Is 30:18; 40:31. Many of our questions and concerns will not be understood till we enter the sanctuary of God Ps 73:16,17.

The LORD'S Answer

2:2-3 **The revelation of God's eternal truth** God's purpose has been determined since before the foundation of the world Acts 17:26,27. He works out everything in conformity with the purpose of his will Eph 1:11. Nothing stops him from carrying out his plan Is 14:26,27. He reveals truth as it is required and ensures that his purpose is fulfilled. We can be assured that God does answer our prayer 1Jn 5:14,15.

The Almighty was about to reveal a foundational truth to Habakkuk v3.

2:4 The righteous will live by his faith As the problem of evil was pursued the basis for individual righteousness was stated. The Bible explains that we all stand condemned before God. No one is righteous Is 64:6. No one will be declared righteous in God's sight by observing the Law Rom 3:20 - for that would require keeping the whole Law at all times Jas 2:10.

God provided a means of righteousness that is **by faith from first to last** - that is apart from deeds and **comes through faith in Jesus to all who believe** Rom 1:17; 3:21,22. God required his Son to die for the sins of the world. When a person believes this truth they are accepted by God as righteous - they have the right to stand in his Presence 2Cor 5:21.

All those who were accepted as righteous in the Old Testament were recognized **because of their faith in God** - they acknowledged God, they believed and responded to what he said - they were looking forward to the fulfillment of God's promises Heb 11:6,13,39,40. God revealed this fundamental truth to Habakkuk six hundred years before the coming of Jesus v4.

2:5-12 Evil Nature Exposed Why is it necessary that mankind come to God in faith? Inherently man is proud, arrogant, self-centered - never satisfied. The heart is deceitful above all things and beyond cure, who can understand it? Jer 17:9. We all have a tendency to do wrong. Under sufficiently adverse circumstances human response is unpredictable Rom 3:9-20. Our character and integrity must be tested to prove it is genuine. Because people choose to live independently from God evil must run its course so that the pride and vanity of sinful human nature is fully exposed - then judgment is assured Jas 1:2-4.

The people of Judah (and fallen Israel) had the knowledge of God and his covenant which they had broken and so they would be punished first. But then the nations of the world would be called to account v12.

2:13-19 The Glory of God All human effort works towards the fulfilment of God's plan. The aspirations of the nations will be brought to nothing. The ultimate result of human history will be that *the earth will be filled with the knowledge of the glory of the LORD v13,14.*

All our questions will be answered when *I will know fully as I am fully known 1Cor 13:12.* The violence people have done will be returned upon them - idols and philosophies of the world will be proved to be of no benefit v18,19.

2:20 The LORD is in His Holy Temple Having been told what could be known Habakkuk was reminded of what he already knew – **let all the earth be silent before him**. There is great joy for those who learn to spend time in the Presence of God Ps 91:1,2,9. This honor was secured for us by Jesus on the cross Heb 10:19-22. As we read and meditate on God's Word and learn to walk in his Presence we come to greater understanding of his truths and purposes as they are revealed more fully to us. This is the intention and benefit of meditating on God's Word day and night Ps 1:2. We find meaning and security in this life and assurance of life in the world to come.

The knowledge of the sovereignty of God and his ultimate purpose for us is of great encouragement to those who have come to embrace these truths. Many of the questions we ask are to satisfy our curiosity or to meet our personal needs. Many issues we raise are excuses for not accepting what God has clearly revealed in his Word. This exposes our desire to be independent from God. We must accept the reality of God as he reveals himself to us and get on with the work he has asked us to do Acts 1:6-8; Rom 1:18-20; Eph 2:10.

3:1-16 **The Response to Answered Prayer** Having received an answer from God the first response is to be in awe of God's greatness – his awesome deeds v1-3 and power v4-15. Habakkuk was excited and wanted to see God's deeds in his own day. We sometimes forget that the God of miracles is the same today as yesterday Heb 13:8. We need to use our faith to become involved in what God is doing in our circle of influence v2. As in the past God calls us to take him at his Word by trusting him and stepping out in faith Heb 11:2,3. Then we will see him at work.

The second response is to pray for the purposes of God being worked out in our families, churches, nation and world. Habakkuk's fresh revelation of the greatness of God at work in the world made him excited as he saw the outcome of world events in a new light and committed to work expectantly and contentedly as he watched them unfold v16.

3:17-19 Yet I will rejoice in the LORD As we wait on God we find joy in the assurance of his provision. Though we may go through difficult circumstances we know that our faith will be tested to prove that it is genuine 1Pet 1:6-9. We find victory by giving thanks in all circumstances, not because of the situation but because it is God's will that we always be thankful 1Thes 5:16-19. In this way we express our confidence and trust in God and his Holy Spirit fills us with joy and power to live and serve Rom 15:13.

This can only come about as we learn to rejoice 'in the LORD' Phil 4:4. We are so dependent on physical comfort and sense of material wellbeing that these things replace our relationship with God. However as we seek God and grow in our knowledge and experience of him our ability to rejoice in him develops Eph 5:18-21.

Habakkuk shows us the path -

> *The Sovereign LORD is my strength –*
> *he makes my feet like the feet of a deer,*
> *he enables me to go on the heights v18,19.*

Zephaniah – 'hidden of YHWH'

Introduction – Samaria the capital of Israel was conquered and the people dispersed among the nations one hundred years before Zephaniah prophesied. Josiah was a good king in Judah who introduced reforms but they were not long lasting as immediately after his death there were four evil kings over twenty-three years leading to the fall of Jerusalem in 586 BC 2Kin 22 to 24.

Author – Zephaniah, prophet of Judah. He was of the royal line of Judah 1:1.

Period – In the reign of Josiah around 625 BC before the fall of Jerusalem – he was a contemporary of Jeremiah and Nahum.

Theme – **God's righteous nature is revealed in history** and includes the demand for discipline and correction as seen through the ages. Those who have followed justice and mercy have prospered. Those who were self-reliant and evil eventually have fallen 1:6. It was time for Judah to experience discipline because they ignored God and did not follow his ways. The same principles apply on a national and personal scale today.

The Great Day of the LORD will come in the end time when *the whole world will be consumed by the fire of my jealous anger 3:8.*

The Reason for the Creation God will gather a redeemed and transformed people to share his glory in eternity 3:9,16,17.

THE GREAT DAY OF THE LORD

1:1-3 **The Sovereignty of God** A warning was given that all people will be accountable before the holiness of God.

1:4-13 **A Time of Reckoning** Judah followed a similar path to Samaria turning away from the LORD. They turned their backs on God and worshiped foreign idols. They were complacent, believing that God was not involved in their lives - *who think 'the LORD will do nothing, either good or bad' v12.* Although they saw God's judgment on Samaria and had been surrounded by foreign armies they continued to live self-centered lives without regard for God and his ways.

1:14-18 **The Great Day of the LORD** While this warning came primarily in regard to the judgment that would come on Judah so there is the long range forecast of the time of reckoning that will occur for all - *he will make a sudden end of all who live in the earth v18*; 2Cor 5:10; Heb 9:27.

2:1-3 Seek righteousness, seek humility; perhaps you will be sheltered on the day of the LORD's anger. Despite the pending disaster the invitation to turn from independence and self-centeredness and to seek God was extended to the people. This offer is still available to the individual and nations of our day.

2:4-15 **Judgment of the Nations** The righteous God will call the nations to account as he did his chosen people of old.

Philistia – The cities of the Philistines will be left in ruins v4. The land will be returned to the remnant of the house of Judah. The LORD will care for his people and restore their fortunes v7.

Moab and Ammon – The nations to the east and south east of Judah will be judged for their disregard for God's people, for their pride, insults and mocking v8. In the end time all nations will give account for their independence from God v11.

Cush – the people in Upper Egypt will be punished v12.

Assyria – the nation that conquered the northern kingdom of Israel will be judged, left in ruins v13. This seemed incredible at the time but occurred some ten years later in 612 BC v15.

3:1-4 **The Case Against God's People** From the start the ten tribes that made up the northern kingdom of Israel tuned away from God - they immediately established independence, adopted idols and lived by worldly standards 1Kin 12:25-30. Over a period of 208 years all of their 19 kings were evil.

Judah in the south retained the capital at Jerusalem and the Temple. They maintained the royal line of David. Of their 20 kings over 344 years, 8 were good. Despite this the people generally followed the idols and standards of the world as well. They became rebellious and defiled – accepting no correction. They did not trust God or draw near to him, profaning the Temple and breaking God's law.

3:5 **God's Righteous Nature** Although the people had failed God he dealt with them righteously. He does no wrong! We must recognize this revealed aspect of the nature of God Deu 32:4; Jas 1:17. This truth gives us the confidence and trust that every circumstance will be worked out for our good Eph 2:10.

His justice was available each day without fail. Part of the goodness of God includes the demand for discipline and correction. When he acts it will be at the right time.

3:6-8 **The Day of the LORD** will come at the end time. The people do not fear the LORD or accept correction v7. *The whole world will be consumed by the fire of my jealous anger v8.*

THE PURPOSE OF CREATION
3:9-15 **The Remnant from all ages** While this passage considers the future restoration and blessing of Judah it also looks forward to God's ultimate plan to preserve a people for himself from the nations -
• they will have purified lips *that call on the name of the LORD and serve him shoulder to shoulder v9* – made possible by the filling of the Holy Spirit Jer 31:33
• the shame of sin will be removed from them v11 – made possible by the sacrificial death of Jesus 1Pet 1:18-20
• they will not be proud and arrogant but meek and humble v12
• they will be a redeemed and transformed people, who trust in the name of the LORD v13
• they will shout aloud, be glad and rejoice with all their hearts for the LORD the King will be with them v14,15.
Many of the verses in the Prophets will only be fulfilled in the messianic millennium kingdom 2:7,11; 3:8-12.

3:16-20 **The LORD Will Rejoice** We can only be amazed at the wonder of God's plan of salvation for the world. In that day *he will take great delight in you - he will rejoice over you with singing v17.*
This is the reason for the creation – so that God will bless those who embrace his love and favor. He is gathering a people from all nations *that in the coming ages he might show the incomparable riches of his grace expressed in his kindness toward us in Christ Jesus Eph 2:7.*
All things will be put right – all things made new Rev 21:5.
Who can forego this offer?

Haggai – 'festive'

Introduction – The captives from Judah were in exile from the fall of Jerusalem in 586 BC until Babylon was conquered by the Medes and Persians in 539 BC. Cyrus II king of Persia 559–530 BC gave the exiled people the opportunity to return to Jerusalem. The first to return were a group of 50,000 under the leadership of Zerubbabel (of the royal line of the kings of Judah and rebuilder of the Temple) and Joshua (priest and later high priest). Work began on the foundations of the Temple by 536 BC but stopped due to local resistance Ezr 3:8. Sixteen years later the work was still not progressing. Haggai and Zechariah had returned with this group and now encouraged them to continue with the work. The prophecies began in 520 BC and the Temple was dedicated 4 years later in 516 BC.

Author – Haggai, the prophet in exile who returned to Jerusalem.

Period – Haggai and Zechariah were prophets under Persian rule probably born in captivity and who both returned to Jerusalem in 538 BC Ezr 5:1; 6:14.

Theme – The Priority of the LORD's Work in rebuilding the Temple
The Jews returning from exile built their own homes and were settling down to self-centered lives. It was time to focus on God's work of rebuilding the Temple. Then the people would receive the blessing of the LORD in their lives.

Time to Build the Temple

1:1 The first prophecy was in 520 BC (second year of Darius 522-486 BC). The exiles had been back in Judah for seventeen years. Zerubbabel was appointed governor of Judah 2:2. Joshua, son of Jehozadak the high priest seemed to officiate.

1:2-15 **Give careful thought to your ways** To the people of Judah (and all Israel in the time of the United Kingdom) the Temple represented the Presence of God - it was built to bring honor to God. As the people returned to Jerusalem from the exile they continued in their self-centered ways forgetting God and living for themselves.

They had rebuilt their homes and re-established their gardens, yet the Temple remained in ruin. Their crops were not producing and they lacked prosperity. They were told *'give careful thought to your ways'* *v7* – advice for all ages. The Lord takes pleasure in our commitment and is honored by our devotion and service v8. When we neglect the LORD and his work we are left to our own devices – he withdraws his blessing. God uses the circumstances of life to test our faith and gain our attention v10,11.

When we respond to God's leading his Holy Spirit **stirs up within us** and we prosper, both in our personal lives and in our service v13. Jesus confirmed this as the way of life for us under the New Covenant - *do not worry about your life* (be anxious about nothing) - *but seek first his kingdom and his righteousness and all these things will be given to you as well Mt 6:25-34.* This is advice we fail to follow to our disadvantage!

2:1-9 **The Glory of the New** The people responded to the call and six weeks later, as the work was under way further encouragement was given. The Spirit of God would remain with the people as he had covenanted with them when they came out of Egypt v5. God will once more shake the heavens and earth and all nations. The glory of the new will be greater than the former glory. God will grant peace. These prophecies relate to the coming of the Holy Spirit at Pentecost. They also refer to the end time when Jesus will return - all creation will be shaken and all things will be renewed Heb 12:26,27.

2:10-19 **From this day I will bless you** Two months later another prophecy was given – the people had suffered greatly because of their sins and rejection of the LORD. This defilement separated them from the holy God. They were now cleansed by the discipline of the exile and had a new start. They could once again expect to receive God's blessing. We look forward to the complete fulfilment of this prophecy in the eternal kingdom Rev 22:1-5.

God's Chosen One

2:20-23 **The New Kingdom** Zerubbabel was leader of the people, governor of Judah and master rebuilder of the Temple. God chose him to be his representative to bring prosperity to the people. He was of the royal line of David 1Chr 3:17-19. The signet ring refers to having God's authority. Zerubbabel was a prefigure of Jesus, the coming king.

This is a prophetic word referring to the end time millennium reign when Jesus Christ will rule on the throne of David and all nations will submit to his reign of peace Is 9:7; Lk 1:32.

Zechariah – 'YHWH remembers'

Introduction – The majority of captives from Judah were in exile from the final siege and fall of Jerusalem in 586 BC. Babylon was conquered by the Medes and Persians in 539 BC. Cyrus II king of Persia 559–530 BC gave the exiled people the opportunity to return to Jerusalem. Zechariah the prophet returned with Haggai and the first party in 538 BC. They began their prophecies in 520 BC and the Temple was dedicated four years later in 516 BC.

Author – Zechariah, prophet in exile who returned to Jerusalem.

Period – Haggai and Zechariah were prophets under Persian rule probably born in captivity and both returned to Jerusalem in 538 BC Ezr 5:1; 6:14.

Theme – **God's Purposes** The people from exile built their own homes and were settling down to self-centered lives. It was time to focus on God's work of rebuilding the Temple. Then the people would receive the blessing of the LORD in their lives.

Eight Visions of the Future While there was current application these were long term prophecies relating to future world events involving all mankind and the **Coming of the Messiah**.

The Coming King and Universal Eternal Kingdom There will be a new order where God will dwell with his people.

This Book gives the most clear Messianic and end time prophecies of the Old Testament.

SUMMARY
Time to Build the Temple 1:1-6
Eight Visions of the Future 1:7 to 6:8
The Messiah - the Priest King 6:9 to 9:8
The Coming King - a long range prophecy 9:9 to 13:9
The Universal Eternal Kingdom 14:1-21

Time to Build the Temple
1:1-6 **The Need for Faithfulness** The year of the first prophecy was 520 BC, second year of Darius, two months after Haggai's encouragement for the people to focus on rebuilding of the Temple Hag 1:1. Zechariah reminded them of the evil practices that had caused the downfall of Jerusalem Hag 1:2-15.

The people recognized their wrongdoing, repented and returned to the work of rebuilding the Temple.

EIGHT VISIONS OF THE FUTURE Three months later Zechariah saw eight visions which applied to Judah and also spoke of the end time of the world. They are progressive.

1:7-17 **Vision 1 - God's Favor on His People - Judgment on the Nations** Having punished his people for their sin and rebellion by the years in exile it would be expected that the righteous, just and holy God would bring judgment on the people of the world. The vision involved a man on a horse with other riders standing among trees. The myrtle was a common tree representing Israel. The riders went into the world and reported back to their leader that the world was at rest and in peace – living independent, self-centered lives and ignoring God. He had become very angry with his people v2 - so his anger would rise against the people of the world v15. There will be a final judgment Rev 20:11-15.
God will re-establish Jerusalem in peace and prosperity v17. This prophecy has fulfilment in the present day and in the climax in the end time!

1:18-21 **Vision 2 - Restoration of Judah** Four horns represented kings of Assyria (Tiglath-Pileser III and Shalmaneser V) who scattered Israel and of Babylon (Sennacherib and Nebuchadnezzar) who scattered Judah and Jerusalem 2Kin 15:19; 17:3; 18:13; 25:1. Four craftsmen builders would restore Jerusalem and Judah - Zerubbabel, Joshua, Ezra and Nehemiah.

2:1-13 **Vision 3 - Future of Zion** The present city was being rebuilt. This vision refers to the future when God will live with his people, the apple of his eye, in the new Jerusalem - a city without walls. Babylon will be plundered v9. *Many nations will be joined with the LORD in that day and will become my people v11.* This is his plan for creation. The world will stand in awe of the Sovereign God when this is achieved v13; Rev 21:3.

3:1-7 **Vision 4 - Forgiveness of Sin** By this time Joshua was appointed high priest Hag 1:1. This vision represented all those who are being accused continually before God by Satan Rev 12:10. The accuser is silenced v2. Joshua was rescued from the world (a burning stick snatched from the fire) and cleansed – his filthy clothes were taken and replaced with rich garments Is 61:10. If he walked in God's ways he will govern God's house.

3:8-10 The Coming Messiah Joshua was *symbolic of things to come! v8.* The name Joshua (Hebrew *Jeshua*) equates with Jesus meaning 'the LORD saves' v9; Mt 1:21. This forgiveness, cleansing and royal appointment could only be accomplished by the Messiah (God's Servant, **the Branch**) – Jesus Christ - who *was slain and with his blood purchased people from every nation and made them to be a kingdom and priests - to reign on earth Rev 5:9,10.* The matchless grace of God and high calling of all his saints are beyond understanding! Jesus is the stone that causes men to stumble (those who will not accept him as Savior and LORD). He will remove sin forever on that day when he returns to reign v9,10; 10:4; Is 28:16; 1Pet 2:6; Mk 12:10.

4:1-14 Vision 5 - God Works Among His People The lampstand with seven lights represented the people of God, seven being the number of perfection v2; Rev 1:12,20. In this case it referred to rebuilding the Temple but the principle applies to all generations. The two olive trees pour out golden oil representing the work of the Holy Spirit through prayer.

'Not by might, nor by power, but by my Spirit,' says the LORD Almighty v6 The message to Zerubbabel was that his success in rebuilding the Temple would not depend on worldly ability or methods. **God's Holy Spirit accomplishes his purposes** through those who know his Presence and follow his direction - this is the Word to all who would respond to the work of the LORD Gal 5:25. Without his guidance the work is in vain Ps 127:1. Under his leadership the work will prosper – mountains of obstacles will become level ground v7. Zerubbabel was assured that as he had begun the work so his hands would complete it under God's provision v9. The Temple was completed and dedicated four years later in 516 BC. **The Day of Small Beginnings** v10 When we depend on the LORD we are empowered to do what he asks. We are not discouraged by outward appearance or slow progress. Perseverance is required in all we do Mt 15:33-38; Jas 1:2-4. The seven eyes symbolize God's omniscient knowledge of all people and activities v10.

The Power, Privilege and Purpose of Prayer The two olive trees providing oil represent those who are appointed to serve (stand by) the LORD. This reinforces the importance and power of prayer behind the efforts of Zerubbabel and Joshua v14. We must apply this principle in all things 1Tim 2:1-4.

5:1-4 **Vision 6 - Individual Sin will be Judged** The flying scroll shows that every person will be required to give account of every thought, word and deed Mt 12:36. It is symbolic of the 'books of deeds' and contrasts with the Lamb's 'book of life' Dan 12:1; Rev 20:12-15. Human conscience demands that people be held accountable.

5:5-11 **Vision 7 – The Sin of Nations will be Judged** The woman is the personification of evil deeds associated with Babylon from the beginning and representing world government in the end time Gen 10:10; 11:2,9. The measuring basket signifies judgment of sin in the nations Rev 17:3; 18:2.

6:1-8 **Vision 8 – God's purposes** Four chariots went through the earth to survey and progress world affairs similar to the horsemen in 1:7-17 who had only a reporting function. They may be compared to the four horsemen sent out into the world by *the LORD of the whole earth* to initiate the end time events after the opening of the sealed scroll by Jesus Rev 6:1-8.

THE MESSIAH - The Priest King
After the eight visions prophetic insight was given of the One who would fulfill God's plan for mankind.

6:9-15 **A Symbol of the Future** Zechariah was told to crown Joshua the high priest as symbolic of One who would come to build the Temple of the LORD. He would have the title '**Branch**' and be a **priest on his throne**, combining kingship with priesthood, harmonizing the two roles v9-12.

Joshua had already symbolized the **Branch** who would **remove sin in a day** 3:8,9. The **Branch** of the stump of Jesse was foretold 280 years before this by Isaiah Is 11:1. *The LORD will raise up for David a righteous Branch, and he shall reign as king and deal wisely and shall execute justice and righteousness in the land Jer 23:5; 33:15.*

Jesus is identified as the Branch of the line of David who is High Priest and King and will remove sin in a day Lk 1;32,33.

6:15 **The Future Temple** Zerubbabel was already confirmed as the one who would finish the present Temple under reconstruction 4:9. So there must be another temple in mind.

There are a number of temples described in the Bible -
- **Solomon's Temple** – dedicated 959 BC, destroyed 586 BC
- **Zerubbabel's Temple** – dedicated 516 BC, defiled 169 BC
- **Herod's Temple** – began 19 BC and destroyed AD 70
- **Temple of the Holy Spirit** – the current experience of the believer 1Cor 6:19; 2Cor 6:16; 1Pet 2:5
- **City of God** - the Presence of the LORD God Almighty and the Lamb - there will be no Temple there! Rev 21:22
- **Tribulation Temple** – Mt 24:15; 2Thes 2:4. This applied to Herod's Temple destroyed by Rome in AD 70. It also refers to the final tribulation where the temple (shrine) symbolizes the people of God in the end time Rev 11:1-2
- **Temple of the LORD** – to be established by the Messiah, the Branch refers to the fulfilment of the age when the remnant of both Covenants will be united in the Millennium City by Jesus when he returns (Zechariah's future Temple) 6:12-15; Is 2:2-4; Ezk 40:1 to 42:20. As with Ezekiel, Zechariah saw the future in terms of the restoration of the physical Temple.

6:15 **The warning to diligently obey God** foresaw the future disobedience and departure of the people from the LORD and further judgment confirming the need for a Savior of mankind Mal 1:6; 2:11. It also refers to the need for all mankind, both Jew and Gentile to respond to the Gospel of Jesus Christ to receive eternal life Acts 2:38,39; Rom 10:10-13.

7:1-10 **Action Rather than Ritual** Two years later in the fourth year of Darius the people inquired about the rituals they should keep. They were told that obeying God's laws was what was important – justice, mercy and compassion, care for the oppressed and poor. Good thoughts and actions were pleasing to God - not formal outward show.

7:11-13 **The Current Condition** - Those who turn their backs and stop their ears cannot expect to receive Gods' blessing - *when I called they did not listen; so when they called I would not listen v13.*

8:1-24 **Prosperity for God's People in Jerusalem** God's love for his chosen people, faithful ones of the Old Testament and Jerusalem has not changed v1. A remnant from many nations has returned to Israel today and receive God's blessing v20. The day will come when Jerusalem will play a special part in world history. Peoples of many nations will come to dwell there for the LORD is concerned with all people v21-23; Mic 4:2; Rev 14:1.

9:1-8 Judgment was pronounced on surrounding nations - Syria, Damascus, Tyre, Sidon and Philistia - all conquered by Alexander 331 BC (190 years after the prediction) - *for now I am keeping watch v8.*

THE COMING KING – a long range prophecy

9:9-13 **A New King in Jerusalem** He will be righteous, humble and having salvation v9. Jesus fulfilled this prophecy at his Triumphal Entry into Jerusalem when he allowed the people to declare him king Mt 21:1-5. *He will proclaim peace to the nations; his rule will extend - to the ends of the earth v10.*

9:14-17 **The Trumpet Sound** The kingdom will be completed when the Sovereign LORD sounds the trumpet v14 at the Second Coming of Jesus Mt 24:30,31.

10:1-12 Surely I will redeem them v8 God gives rain, sunshine and plants of the field to all according to his grace and mercy. *From Judah will come the cornerstone v4* So the house of Judah will be redeemed by the Lion of the tribe of Judah, the Root of David Rev 5:5.

11:1-17 **The Shepherd Priest and King** Judgment would come on those who reject the new king especially the leaders in Israel who were appointed as shepherds of the people but proved unfaithful v4-6. This occurred under the Roman generals - Titus in AD 70 and Hadrian in AD 135 v15-17.

Zechariah was called to act out the role of a faithful shepherd v7. He took two staffs, representing God's blessing and provision, one called 'Faithful' meaning God's grace and one called 'Union' meaning unity between Israel and Judah. Both were then broken showing God's disfavor v10,14.

11:7-13 **Jesus is the Good Shepherd** Jn 10:11 The Good Shepherd would come and they would detest him paying thirty pieces of silver for him which would be used to purchase the potter's field v8,12,13. So the Old Covenant would be revoked for a New Covenant v10. He was betrayed for thirty pieces of silver - used to buy the potter's field Mt 27:3-10. He enacted the New Covenant which is open to all nations Mt 26:26-28.

12:1-9 **The Final Battle** The Sovereign LORD Creator of the heavens and earth, *who forms the spirit of man within him* will bring about the culmination of world history v1-3. Jerusalem will be oppressed by all nations on earth. They will return to dependence on God and will be defended by God v9 - it will be the time of Jacob's trouble Jer 30:7-10; Rev 20:9.

12:10-14 **Messiah Accepted** The Holy Spirit will be poured out on Jerusalem and *they will look on me, the one they have pierced* in repentance v10. Zechariah, in common with other prophets foresaw the eventual acceptance of the Messiah by the Jewish people and the restoration of Jerusalem Rom 11:25-27.

13:1-9 **Cleansing from Sin** God's chosen people will be cleansed from sin and impurity. Jesus received wounds from the house of his friends v6.

13:7-9 **The Good Shepherd Struck** Jesus is the shepherd that was struck - in order for sins to be forgiven v7; Is 53:4; Mt 26:31. The chosen remnant will be refined like silver and tested like gold v9.

They will call on his name and he will answer them. He will say *'They are my People,' and they will say, 'the LORD is our God' v9*; Rev 21:3.

THE UNIVERSAL ETERNAL KINGDOM

14:1-5 **The Day of the LORD** Although the people would be judged for their rejection of the Good Shepherd v1,2; 11:4-6 the LORD will bring about deliverance. The Messiah will stand on the Mount of Olives to defend Jerusalem and fight against the nations v3,4; Rev 14:1.

Then the LORD my God will come, and all the holy ones with him v5. The 'holy ones' are also called 'saints'. There are over 30 references to 'saint' in the O T - apart from Dan 7:18,21,25; 8:13; 22:27 (including Deu 33:2,3; Job 5:1; Ps 16:3; 30:4; 31:23; 34:9; 106:16; Prov 2:8; 1Sam 2:9; 2Chr 6:41; Hos 11:12 and Zech 14:5).

14:6-21 **The Millennium Rule** The day of the LORD will usher in a new order. This is the foretold millennium reign Ezk 39:1-29; Rev 20:4-6. Living water will flow out of Jerusalem v8 Jn 7:37-39; Rev 22:1.

The LORD will be King over the whole earth v9. People from all nations will come to worship the King v16. Jerusalem will be **'Holy to the LORD'** v20; Is 65:17-25; Mic 4:1-8.

After this will be established the **Eternal Kingdom of God** - revealed in more detail to John Rev 21:1-3; 26,27.

Malachi – 'My messenger'

Introduction – Malachi was the last of the writing prophets in the Old Testament before the 400 silent years leading up to the coming of Jesus. He spoke in a time of religious decline. After the return to Jerusalem from exile in Babylon in 538 BC the Temple was rebuilt and dedicated in 516 BC. Ezra the priest returned in 458 BC to carried out reforms restoring the Temple worship and reinstating the Law. Nehemiah returned in 445 BC and after 15 years working with Ezra the walls and city were rebuilt and secured. National and religious reforms were introduced Neh 13:1-31. Malachi made no reference to these fellow countrymen.

The people had returned from exile with high expectations of prosperity and the coming of the Messiah. After 100 years they were becoming disillusioned again and many turned away from God 3:14. Malachi told them the reason for their hardships was their rejection of God and his ways 2:8.

Author – Malachi the prophet of Israel after the return from exile.

Period – In a time of religious decline possibly after 430 BC.

Theme - The New Covenant The contrast of God's love for his people and the frailty of human nature showed the need of a Savior and transformation of the human heart by the coming Messiah heralded by John the Baptist.

SUMMARY
God's Plan for Mankind 1:1 to 2:9
Judah Unfaithful - the Marriage Covenant 2:10-16
The Covenants 2:17
A New Covenant 3:1-5
Independence from God 3:6-18
The New Covenant Announced 4:1-6
The Silent Years

GOD'S PLAN FOR MANKIND
1:1-5 **God's Choice** The people were reminded that as the descendants of Jacob they were the chosen people of God. Esau his older brother had despised his birthright and although he became forefather of the nation of Edom it was Jacob who became patriarch of the people of Israel Gen 25:34; 32:28. Hate for Esau served to emphasize the magnitude of God's

love for his chosen people. We see this love for us in the death of Jesus Christ Rom 5:8.

1:6-14 **Human Response** God had acted as a father to the people and looked for respect. But they were treating him with contempt v6. Their offerings were defiled and their religious formality was not acceptable. They did not honor God or his name. They saw service as a burden. God prepared to 'shut the Temple doors'! v10.

God's ultimate plan is *that my name will be great among the nations from the rising to the setting of the sun v11.* The day will come when prayer, genuine reverence and service will be offered from sincere hearts by people from all nations.

2:1-9 **Unfaithful Priests** The responsibility of the priest as messenger of the LORD was to maintain knowledge of God and his ways and to instruct the people. But in addition to false teaching they were practicing injustice and partiality. How quickly they had reverted to the old ways. Judgment on the descendants of the priests and people occurred when Jerusalem was plundered in AD 70.

JUDAH UNFAITHFUL

2:10-16 **A Symbol of Unfaithfulness** The triune God - Father Son and Holy Spirit desires relationship with his people and that they should act towards each other with respect. This was expounded by Jesus in the 'high priestly prayer' v10; Jn 17:1-26.

The Marriage Covenant is the institution ordained by God between man and woman for the procreation and upbringing of children Gen 2:20-25. So broken relationship in marriage means profaning the covenant one has made with God v14.

Has not the LORD made them one? In flesh and spirit they are his v15 God hates divorce because it means failure of two people to honor their word to each other and before God. He seeks godly offspring from parents that honor him and uphold their covenant with him. Divorce is a symbol of broken relationship with God. The violence of man is hated as well - who walk away from the commitments and obligations to family under God v16.

So guard yourself in your spirit, and do not break faith v16 – God is Spirit and we must honor him from within (with our spirit).

THE COVENANTS

***2:17* Broken Covenants** The people had wearied the LORD by condoning evil practices in God's name and blaming God for their misfortunes when they themselves were responsible. They had broken the Covenant with him.

God has made many Covenants with mankind -

- **Man** - the Covenant of fellowship, provision and residence in Eden Gen 2:15
- **Adam** - promise of a Redeemer (seed of woman) Gen 3:15
- **Noah** - God's wrath reserved for the end time Gen 8:21,22
- **Abraham** - All nations of the earth will be blessed through his descendants Gen 12:2,3
- **David** - An eternal kingdom through his descendents 2Sam 7:16

God made a number of Covenants with Israel through Moses -

- **Covenant at Sinai** – God chose Israel out of all nations to be his treasured possession, and a holy nation Ex 19:5. They refused this relationship and requested that Moses act as mediator Ex 20:18-21
- **Covenant of the Book** – Israel were God's people and he would bless them so long as they kept the Law as required in the Book of the Covenant – principally the Ten Commandments Ex 24:7,8. They continually failed the conditions and lost their nationhood
- **Covenant of a Lasting Priesthood** - Aaron and the Levites were to faithfully serve before God and teach the people the requirements of the Law Num 25:12,13. It was this Covenant of the Priesthood that God now accused them of breaking v8
- **A New Covenant Foreshadowed** – *The time is coming, declares the LORD when I will **make a new covenant** - I will put my law in their minds and write it on their hearts. I will be their God and they will be my people* - sin will be forgiven and each person will have a personal relationship with God Jer 31:31-34. *By calling this covenant 'new' he made the first one obsolete and what is obsolete and aging will soon disappear Heb 8:13.*

THE NEW COVENANT DESCRIBED

***3:1-5* The Coming Messiah** Because the priests and people violated the Old Covenant God was ready to introduce the **New Covenant -**

- *I will send my messenger who will prepare the way before me v1* – John the Baptist fulfilled this prophecy announcing the coming of the Messiah Is 40:3-5; Lk 3:4-6
- *Suddenly the Lord you are seeking will come to his Temple v1* – they were seeking the Messiah - he came as Jesus Christ Mt 1:16; 21:1,2-5
- *The LORD Almighty v1* spoke these words declaring the deity of the Messiah. Jesus was declared as God's Son and Person of the Trinity Jn 1:1-14; Col 1:15-20
- *The messenger of the Covenant v1* – the priests were messengers of God so the Messiah would be God's messenger of the New Covenant
- *He will be like a refiner's fire v2* – Jesus purged the Temple and pronounced judgment on the religious authorities Jn 2:13-17; Mt 5:20
- *He will purify the Levites and refine them like gold and silver v3.* The purification referred to could only come by a perfect sacrifice Heb 7:27,28. Jesus did away with sacrifice by his death on the cross – making perfect forever those who are being made holy Heb 10:14
- *Then the LORD will have people who bring offerings in righteousness v3.* These members of the New Covenant will be *a chosen people, a royal priesthood, a holy nation, a people belonging to God – called - to declare the praises of him who called you out of darkness into his wonderful light 1Pet 2:9,10.* They will be his treasured possession, a kingdom of priests and a holy nation offering spiritual sacrifices of praise acceptable to God through Jesus Christ Ex 19:5,6.

Independence From God

3:6-15 The Immutable Nature of God Declared He does not change – neither his holiness, his love nor his mercy. Also his plan for the salvation of mankind will not be thwarted v6; Is 14:26,27. From the beginning Jacob (Israel) had turned away from God's decrees and did not kept them v6. Even so he continued to call them to return to him and receive his blessing. Now they had demonstrated the depth of their rebellion – they no longer gave offerings of thankfulness to him. By holding back the tithes and offerings they indicated their disregard for God v9. He challenged them to 'test him' in faith and *see if I will not throw open the floodgates of heaven and pour out so much blessing that you will not have room enough for it v10.*

The extent of their rejection was expressed in the harsh things they said against God – *It is futile to serve God. What did we gain by carrying out his requirements – evildoers prosper and even those who challenge God escape v14-15.* This attitude is taken by many today.

3:16-18 **The New Remnant** The new people will fear the LORD and call on him. A scroll was written with the names of those past, present and future who feared the LORD and honored his name Rev 20:15. They will be his new 'treasured possession' and will enter into a relationship with him as **Father with sons** v17. There will be distinction between the righteous and the wicked, between those who serve God and those who do not.

THE NEW COVENANT ANNOUNCED

4:1-3 **The Son of Righteousness** The Day of the LORD will bring judgment. Those who are arrogant and do evil will be separated from God. But for those who revere his name they will see the Messiah – he will heal from sin, from sickness and disease. Those who accept him will be filled with the joy of salvation Is 12:3. Then in the end time evil will be abolished and the Messiah will reign in holiness and peace Rev 20:10; 21:3-5.

4:4 **Messiah Foretold in the Old Covenant -**
• Jesus showed the disciples how the Books of Moses and the Prophets foretelling the coming of the Messiah spoke of him Lk 24:25-27
• Jesus explained that everything must be fulfilled that is written about him in the Law of Moses, the Prophets and the Psalms – that the Christ must suffer and rise from the dead on the third day and that repentance and forgiveness of sins will be preached in his name to all nations beginning at Jerusalem Lk 24:44-47.
There are some 300 Old Testament prophecies that were fulfilled during the first coming of Jesus. There are still many to be fulfilled at his Second Coming
• Jesus told the leaders of his day that the Scriptures testify about him Jn 5:39
• Jesus confirmed to the Samaritan woman at the well that he is the Messiah Jn 4:25,26
• The apostle Paul, an expert in the Old Testament Scriptures confirmed that the Gospel is in accordance with the Scriptures – *that Christ died for our sins according to the Scriptures, that he was buried, that he was raised on the third day according to the Scriptures 1Cor 15:3-7*

- Jesus did not come to abolish the Law or the Prophets but to fulfill them Mt 5:17,18.

4:5 The Prophets Moses and Elijah The two great miracle working prophets of the Old Testament were Moses and Elijah. Malachi declared that a prophet like Elijah would prepare the way for the Messiah. The Messiah would also be a prophet like Moses Deu 18:15,18 -

- John the Baptist was the prophet like Elijah. This was acknowledged by Jesus Mt 17:11,12; Mk 9:11-13
- Jesus is the prophet, priest and king who was foretold by Moses
- As Moses was the mediator of the Old Covenant so Jesus is the mediator of the New Covenant Heb 9:15; 12:24
- Jesus first announced that he was the Messiah (called Christ) to the woman of Samaria Jn 4:25,26
- Jesus accepted the declaration of Peter that he was the Messiah – the Christ, the Son of the living God Mt 16:16
- It was because Jesus accepted the title of Messiah that he was crucified – this was confirmed by each Gospel writer Mt 26:62-66; Mk 14:62; Lk 22:70,71; Jn 19:7.

4:6 *He will turn the hearts* The role of the Messiah will be to turn the hearts of people to God from all nations of the earth.

THE SILENT YEARS
After the Book of Malachi there were some 400 years of silence of the prophetic word. The next prophet after Malachi and the last of the prophets of the Old Covenant would be John the Baptist who came in the spirit of Elijah to prepare the way for the Messiah, Jesus and the New Covenant.

JUDAH

South Kingdom	Kings	reign BC	
Jerusalem	Rehoboam	930-914	17
344 years	Abijah	913-911	3
*8 kings were good	Asa *	910-870	41
12 knigs were evil			
PROPHETS	Jehoshaphat *	873-849	25
	Jehoram	849-842	8
	Ahaziah	841	
	Athaliah	841-836	6
	Joash *	836-797	40
	Amaziah *	797-768	29
	Azariah *	791-740	52
	(Uzziah)		
Isaiah 740-690 50	Jotham *	751-736	16
Micah 740-700 40	Ahaz	736-721	16
	Hezekiah *	721-693	29
Nahum 622-612 10	Manasseh	693-639	55
Zephaniah 625	Amon	639	
Jeremiah 626-580 46	Josiah *	639-609	31
Joel 600	Jehoahaz	609	
Habakkuk 600	Jehoiakim	608-598	11
Obadiah 586	Jehoiachin	598	
Daniel 605-533 72	Zedekiah	597-586	11
Ezekiel 593-571 22	Fall of Judah 586		390
	(Jerusalem)		
CAPTIVITY	First captives	605	
RETURN	Fall of Babylon	539	
Haggai 520-516 4	First return	538	
Zechariah 520-516 4	Esther	480	
Malachi 430	Ezra	458-430	28
	Nehemiah	445-430	15
SILENT YEARS		400-0	
	Birth of the	LORD JESUS CHRIST	

ISRAEL

Kings	reign BC		North Kingdom	
Jeroboam 1	930-910	22	Samaria	
Nadab	910-909	2	208 years	
Bassha	909-886	24	19 kings were evil	
Elah	886-885	2		
Zimri	885			
Omri	885-874	12	PROPHETS	
Ahab	874-853	22	Elijah	874-852 22
Ahaziah	853-852	2	Elisha	852-798 54
Joram	852-841	12		
Jehu	841-814	28		
Jehoahaz	814-798	17		
Jehoash	798-782	16	Jonah	760
Jeroboam II	793-753	41	Amos	760-750 10
Zechariah	753-752		Hosea	757-722 35
Shallum	752			
Menahem	751-742	10		
Pekahiah	741-740	2		
Pekah	740-732	20		
Hosea	731-722	9		
Fall of Israel 722		241		
(Samaria)				
Fall of Assyria	612			
(Nineveh)				
			Dates indicate start & end of reign unless noted.	
			Reigns of the kings are from the durations in the NIV.	
			Durations involved co-regency and overlap	
After 70 years	605-538			
Temple dedicated	516			
			PROPHETS IN THE DIVIED KINGDOM	

105   Malachi